Approaches to learning and teaching

First Language English

a toolkit for international teachers

Helen Rees-Bidder

Series Editors: Paul Ellis and Lauren Harris

CAMBRIDGE
UNIVERSITY PRESS

University Printing House, Cambridge CB2 8BS, United Kingdom

One Liberty Plaza, 20th Floor, New York, NY 10006, USA

477 Williamstown Road, Port Melbourne, VIC 3207, Australia

314–321, 3rd Floor, Plot 3, Splendor Forum, Jasola District Centre, New Delhi – 110025, India

79 Anson Road, #06–04/06, Singapore 079906

Cambridge University Press is part of the University of Cambridge.

It furthers the University's mission by disseminating knowledge in the pursuit of education, learning and research at the highest international levels of excellence.

www.cambridge.org
Information on this title: www.cambridge.org/9781108406888 (Paperback)

© Cambridge Assessment International Education 2017

First published 2017

20 19 18 17 16 15 14 13 12 11 10 9 8 7 6 5

Printed in Great Britain by CPI Group (UK) Ltd, Croydon CR0 4YY

A catalogue record for this publication is available from the British Library

ISBN 978-1-108-40688-8 Paperback

Contents

Online lesson ideas for this book can be found at
cambridge.org/9781108406888

Acknowledgements

The authors and publishers acknowledge the following sources of copyright material and are grateful for the permissions granted. While every effort has been made, it has not always been possible to identify the sources of all the material used, or to trace all copyright holders. If any omissions are brought to our notice, we will be happy to include the appropriate acknowledgements on reprinting.

Cover image: bgblue/Getty Images; Figure 6.2 Based on 'How I Flipped my Classroom' by Williams, Beth 2013 NNNC Conference, Norfolk Nebraska. Fig 9.1 Cambridge Oracy Skills Framework, University of Cambridge (www.educ.cam.ac.uk/research/projects/oracytoolkit/oracyskillsframework); Fig 11.1 SAMR model is created by Dr Ruben R. Puentedura, *As We May Teach: Educational Technology, From Theory into Practice* (2009); Fig 11.2 Blooms Taxonomy of Technology by Samantha Penney, available under the Creative Commons BY-ND 3.0 licence; Chapter 12 topic 3 includes material adapted from article 'Twenty-five great ideas for teaching current events' by Gary Hopkins for Education World; Fig 12.1 C_Fernandes/Getty Images; Fig 12.3 s0ulsurfing – Jason Swain/Getty Images; Fig 12.4 VCG/VCG via Getty Images; Lesson idea 6.1 James O'Neil/Getty Images; Lesson idea 6.2 Big Cheese Photo/Getty Images

The past paper exam materials used in Chapters 8 and 9, and in Lesson idea 10.1 are reproduced by permission of Cambridge Assessment International Education.

Introduction to the series by the editors

1

1 Approaches to learning and teaching First Language English

This series of books is the result of close collaboration between Cambridge University Press and Cambridge International both departments of the University of Cambridge. The books are intended as a companion guide for teachers, to supplement your learning and provide you with extra resources for the lessons you are planning. Their focus is deliberately not syllabus-specific, although occasional reference has been made to programmes and qualifications. We want to invite you to set aside for a while assessment objectives and grading, and take the opportunity instead to look in more depth at how you teach your subject and how you motivate and engage with your students.

The themes presented in these books are informed by evidence-based research into what works to improve students' learning and pedagogical best practices. To ensure that these books are first and foremost practical resources, we have chosen not to include too many academic references, but we have provided some suggestions for further reading.

We have further enhanced the books by asking the authors to create accompanying lesson ideas. These are described in the text and can be found in a dedicated space online. We hope the books will become a dynamic and valid representation of what is happening now in learning and teaching in the context in which you work.

Our organisations also offer a wide range of professional development opportunities for teachers. These range from syllabus- and topic-specific workshops and large-scale conferences to suites of accredited qualifications for teachers and school leaders. Our aim is to provide you with valuable support, to build communities and networks, and to help you both enrich your own teaching methodology and evaluate its impact on your students.

Each of the books in this series follows a similar structure. In the first chapter, we have asked our authors to consider the essential elements of their subject, the main concepts that might be covered in a school curriculum, and why these are important. The next chapter gives you a brief guide on how to interpret a syllabus or subject guide, and how to plan a programme of study. The authors will encourage you to think too about what is not contained in a syllabus and how you can pass on your own passion for the subject you teach.

The main body of the text takes you through those aspects of learning and teaching which are widely recognised as important. We would like to stress that there is no single recipe for excellent teaching, and that different schools, operating in different countries and cultures, will have strong traditions that should be respected. There is a growing consensus, however, about some important practices and approaches that need to be adopted if students are going to fulfil their potential and be prepared for modern life.

In the common introduction to each of these chapters we look at what the research says and the benefits and challenges of particular approaches. Each author then focuses on how to translate theory into practice in the context of their subject, offering practical lesson ideas and teacher tips. These chapters are not mutually exclusive but can be read independently of each other and in whichever order suits you best. They form a coherent whole but are presented in such a way that you can dip into the book when and where it is most convenient for you to do so.

The final two chapters are common to all the books in this series and are not written by the subject authors. Schools and educational organisations are increasingly interested in the impact that classroom practice has on student outcomes. We have therefore included an exploration of this topic and some practical advice on how to evaluate the success of the learning opportunities you are providing for your students. The book then closes with some guidance on how to reflect on your teaching and some avenues you might explore to develop your own professional learning.

We hope you find these books accessible and useful. We have tried to make them conversational in tone so you feel we are sharing good practice rather than directing it. Above all, we hope that the books will inspire you and enable you to think in more depth about how you teach and how your students learn.

Paul Ellis and Lauren Harris

Series Editors

2 | Purpose and context

International research into educational effectiveness tells us that student achievement is influenced most by what teachers do in classrooms. In a world of rankings and league tables we tend to notice performance, not preparation, yet the product of education is more than just examinations and certification. Education is also about the formation of effective learning habits that are crucial for success within and beyond the taught curriculum.

The purpose of this series of books is to inspire you as a teacher to reflect on your practice, try new approaches and better understand how to help your students learn. We aim to help you develop your teaching so that your students are prepared for the next level of their education as well as life in the modern world.

This book will encourage you to examine the processes of learning and teaching, not just the outcomes. We will explore a variety of teaching strategies to enable you to select which is most appropriate for your students and the context in which you teach. When you are making your choice, involve your students: all the ideas presented in this book will work best if you engage your students, listen to what they have to say, and consistently evaluate their needs.

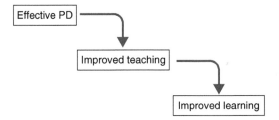

Cognitive psychologists, coaches and sports writers have noted how the aggregation of small changes can lead to success at the highest level. As teachers, we can help our students make marginal gains by guiding them in their learning, encouraging them to think and talk about how they are learning, and giving them the tools to monitor their success. If you take care of the learning, the performance will take care of itself.

When approaching an activity for the first time, or revisiting an area of learning, ask yourself if your students know how to:

- approach a new task and plan which strategies they will use
- monitor their progress and adapt their approach if necessary
- look back and reflect on how well they did and what they might do differently next time.

2 Approaches to learning and teaching First Language English

Effective learners understand that learning is an active process. We need to challenge and stretch our students and enable them to interrogate, analyse and evaluate what they see and hear. Consider whether your students:

- challenge assumptions and ask questions
- try new ideas and take intellectual risks
- devise strategies to overcome any barriers to their learning that they encounter.

As we discuss in the chapters on **Active learning** and **Metacognition**, it is our role as teachers to encourage these practices with our students so that they become established routines. We can help students review their own progress as well as getting a snapshot ourselves of how far they are progressing by using some of the methods we explore in the chapter on **Assessment for Learning**.

Students often view the subject lessons they are attending as separate from each other, but they can gain a great deal if we encourage them to take a more holistic appreciation of what they are learning. This requires not only understanding how various concepts in a subject fit together, but also how to make connections between different areas of knowledge and how to transfer skills from one discipline to another. As our students successfully integrate disciplinary knowledge, they are better able to solve complex problems, generate new ideas and interpret the world around them.

In order for students to construct an understanding of the world and their significance in it, we need to lead students into thinking habitually about why a topic is important on a personal, local and global scale. Do they realise the implications of what they are learning and what they do with their knowledge and skills, not only for themselves but also for their neighbours and the wider world? To what extent can they recognise and express their own perspective as well as the perspectives of others? We will consider how to foster local and global awareness, as well as personal and social responsibility, in the chapter on **Global thinking**.

As part of the learning process, some students will discover barriers to their learning: we need to recognise these and help students to overcome them. Even students who regularly meet success face their own challenges. We have all experienced barriers to our own learning at some point in our lives and should be able as teachers to empathise and share our own methods for dealing with these. In the chapter on **Inclusive education** we discuss how to make learning accessible for everyone and how to ensure that all students receive the instruction and support they need to succeed as learners.

Some students are learning through the medium of English when it is not their first language, while others may struggle to understand subject jargon even if they might otherwise appear fluent. For all students, whether they are learning through their first language or an additional language, language is a vehicle for learning. It is through language that students access the content of the lesson and communicate their ideas. So, as teachers, it is our responsibility to make sure that language isn't a barrier to learning. In the chapter on **Language awareness** we look at how teachers can pay closer attention to language to ensure that all students can access the content of a lesson.

Alongside a greater understanding of what works in education and why, we as teachers can also seek to improve how we teach and expand the tools we have at our disposal. For this reason, we have included a chapter in this book on **Teaching with digital technologies**, discussing what this means for our classrooms and for us as teachers. Institutes of higher education and employers want to work with students who are effective communicators and who are information literate. Technology brings both advantages and challenges and we invite you to reflect on how to use it appropriately.

This book has been written to help you think harder about the impact of your teaching on your students' learning. It is up to you to set an example for your students and to provide them with opportunities to celebrate success, learn from failure and, ultimately, to succeed.

We hope you will share what you gain from this book with other teachers and that you will be inspired by the ideas that are presented here. We hope that you will encourage your school leaders to foster a positive environment that allows both you and your students to meet with success and to learn from mistakes when success is not immediate. We hope too that this book can help in the creation and continuation of a culture where learning and teaching are valued and through which we can discover together what works best for each and every one of our students.

3 | The nature of the subject

Why is English important?

In today's global world, the importance of English has never been greater. It is widely spoken across the world and is the language used in many global businesses and communication systems. Preparing students to speak, read and write fluent English is essential to help them develop as 21st-century learners who can play a role on the world stage. Even more importantly, our students need to develop the thinking skills that will allow them to widen their perspective and become responsible citizens. As an English teacher, you will play an important role in preparing your students for these exciting challenges.

As Eyre & McClure explain in *Curriculum Provision for the Gifted and Talented in the Primary School* (David Fulton Publishers, 2001), English lessons provide opportunities to promote:

*   *moral development*, by exploring questions of right and wrong, values and conflict between values through their reading of fiction and non-fiction, and their discussions and role plays
*   *social development*, by helping students collaborate with others, teaching them the skills necessary to create the effects they wish to achieve when adapting their speech and writing, and through reading, reviewing and discussing texts that present issues and relationships between different groups and between the individual and society in different historical periods and cultures
*   *cultural development*, by helping students explore and reflect on the way that cultures are represented in their stories and poems, and exploring how language relates to national and cultural identities.

Making lessons interesting and challenging is crucial to ensuring that, as an English teacher, you continue to enjoy teaching the subject. Using up-to-date articles about current affairs as a basis for discussion, or topics that will engage teenagers and lead to discursive writing, as well as using the latest technology to support your teaching, will all ensure that you learn and develop alongside your students.

The place of English in the curriculum

As a core subject, English is wide-ranging and eclectic. For English teachers there are both positive and negative aspects to this breadth: teaching a living and evolving language allows teachers to be infinitely creative in their classrooms, but for some there is uncertainty about what precisely defines the nature of the subject. What exactly should English teachers teach?

For many, English teaching is the transference of the teacher's subject knowledge and skills to the students in front of them – the teaching of formal grammar, spelling, vocabulary and literary devices, modelled through reading and practised in the student's own writing. Put simply, English teachers prepare students to make connections between what they read and how they write. Figure 3.1 shows how these connect, with oracy skills developed throughout.

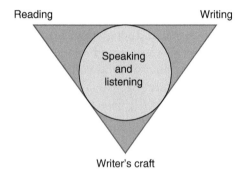

Figure 3.1: Integrating skills development.

Of course, in practice it is far more complicated than this diagram suggests. In the past, English teaching in schools tended to focus on the basic skills of literacy – learning to read and write – and took a more functional view of its place in the curriculum. English has since evolved into a subject that champions 'life-long learning' and the education of a whole person, rather than simply preparing someone for a life of employment. This has led to less emphasis on the formal teaching of standardised handwriting, grammar, spelling and punctuation and more focus on teaching students ways of developing writing skills and making meaning through reading, discussing and analysing a wide range of literary and non-literary texts. In essence, English is an exciting subject to teach because the core of its curriculum is skills-based, leaving the individual teacher with far more freedom to explore their own interests and passions, as well as topical subjects, in the teaching of their subject. Through carefully planned schemes of work exploring a range of topics, English teachers can teach learners to communicate effectively, read with perception and talk convincingly.

One of the core aims of any English teacher is to foster a love of reading in their students and develop their independent reading skills. As examinations test reading comprehension through unseen passages, this is an essential part of the English curriculum. The more students read, the more their own writing skills will develop too.

To encourage reading for pleasure you can:

- Allow and encourage readers to choose their own books when reading for pleasure. To develop a good reading habit it is crucial that reading is enjoyable rather than a chore. Allowing someone to choose their own reading material will ensure that what they choose interests them, and is not too difficult for them. When reading for pleasure, it is beneficial to choose books that do not challenge too greatly as this will develop the habit of reading quickly. If the reader has to decode too many words, their reading becomes stilted and they lose the flow of what they are reading.
- Allow time in lessons for sustained silent reading of the students' chosen books. It's even better if the teacher also reads silently during these times.
- Encourage students to carry a book with them everywhere so that reading for pleasure does not only occur in English lessons. Improving literacy is a whole-school issue.

Teacher Tip

Ask yourself the following questions:

- What does life-long learning mean to you?
- What skills can you teach through English which will be helpful in later life?
- How do you encourage a love of reading in your students?

Developments in the teaching of English

Recent developments in the teaching of English stem from the rapid growth of communication technology in the last two decades. Many decry this development, citing its primary effect as young people reading less fiction, yet research suggests that young people today are reading more rather than less – they are just reading differently. It has also changed the way that we communicate: social media tends to encourage dialogue, brief responses and abbreviated language. Again, this is usually dismissed as 'text-speak' with no relevance in the English classroom, but as these technologies are here to stay, and are likely to become even more sophisticated, we should embrace them and make them an integral part of our teaching. We must teach our students to think about how they adapt their language to communicate in different situations, and also teach them to think about the potential impact and consequences of what they write. Our students are part of a global society like never before and effective communication has never been more significant. We need to teach them skills for the 21st century, where global communication and IT literacy are at the forefront of developments. As English teachers we are able to build this naturally into our curriculum through the topics that we explore, the texts we read and by developing different writing styles in which students can communicate confidently and effectively. The ways in which you can develop your use of digital technologies in the English classroom are explored in Chapter 11 **Teaching with digital technologies**.

🖵 LESSON IDEA ONLINE 3.1: USING NON-FICTION TEXTS

Use this lesson idea as an activity to explore the impact of social media on modern communication. Students can analyse the writer's craft and also discuss how social media is changing the way that we communicate with one another and consider the positive and negative impacts.

How is the English curriculum designed?

Many secondary school English courses divide the English curriculum neatly into the three areas of reading, writing and speaking and listening. This is largely due to the way that the assessment objectives for IGCSE and O Level qualifications are designed. However, most English teachers will approach these three areas in an integrated way in the classroom, as they cannot be separated in terms of skills development and knowledge content, even if they are for purposes of assessment. For example, linking discursive writing to reading passages on the subject being explored allows development of reading skills through analysis of the writer's purpose and choice of language, while ensuring a sound knowledge base of the topic on which to build the student's own views and ideas. Figure 3.2 illustrates the ways that the different assessment areas interlink continuously and stresses the need for a holistic approach to the content of the English curriculum.

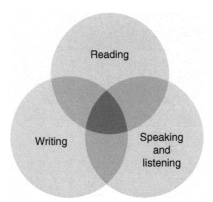

Figure 3.2: The three assessed components in English Language.

English lends itself to collaborative learning, as it is dependent on exchanges of ideas, defending and adapting viewpoints and shared experiences. Studying English in isolation would be unlikely to lead to progress because of the very nature of the subject. It is essential that English teachers embrace the different methods of encouraging active learning to build on student's prior skills and knowledge, and scaffold their learning through carefully planned collaborative activities. Traditional pedagogies often cite group work as being less effective, or a time-filler, but in the English classroom it is an essential tool to ensure progress. Active learning requires highly skilled teaching that uses a wide range of instruction and deep understanding of how assessment can be used effectively to support students at different levels. Ideas about how you can establish active learning in your classroom are explored more fully in Chapter 6 **Active learning**.

Teacher Tip

Using speaking and listening tasks to prepare students for Reading and Writing assessments allows collaborative learning through sharing ideas and experiences, while building a more secure knowledge base. For example, before setting students a discursive writing task, group discussions and presentations on the topic can develop their knowledge and understanding, as well as their awareness of differing viewpoints. The development of oracy skills is discussed in more detail in Chapter 9 **Language awareness**.

Summary

Chapter 3 has focused on the nature of English Language as a subject. Look back over the material presented and reflect on the following questions:

- How fully do you integrate the teaching of reading, writing and speaking and listening in your classroom activities?

- How do you encourage collaborative learning in your classroom?

- How do you develop skills that students need in the 21st century in English lessons?

Key considerations

4

Reflective practice

However long you have been teaching, you never stop learning how to be a better teacher! Reflective practice is the key to successful teaching.

One of the most important lessons that I learnt as I progressed through my career as an English teacher was that examination-led pedagogy can be self-limiting. It is very tempting to teach to the test, and to make students practise past paper after past paper, but all you are really doing is teaching them to pass an examination, rather than develop a rich understanding of the subject itself.

I have also learnt that English skills need to be constructed carefully; for example, asking a student to analyse the way a writer has used language for effect before they can read a text and understand inferred meaning is likely to make them lose confidence in their ability and label themselves a failure. They simply aren't ready to move on to that level of analysis because they have not acquired the level of reading comprehension needed to do the task. It is crucial that as English teachers we differentiate between our students so that we can genuinely take a constructivist approach to developing their skills. This means that lessons need to be planned carefully to ensure that each student is learning at the right level for his or her ability.

Effective Continuous Professional Development (CPD) is a great way of learning about new approaches in the classroom and keeping in touch with the latest developments in educational research. It is important that when you have been on a CPD course, you utilise what you have learnt quickly. Research suggests that if you don't return to the classroom and try out the new ideas and concepts that you have been taught quickly, and reflect on your own practice and its impact on student outcomes, you never will. That is a missed opportunity.

Teacher Tip

When you attend a CPD course, spend some time reflecting on how you will apply what you have learnt to your classroom practice and feed it back to your department as soon as you return to school. You should put your thoughts and ideas down in writing as you look back through the notes that you have made. Think about what you have learnt from the course and ask yourself:

- What will I do next week?
- What will I do next term?
- What will I do next year?

The challenges facing English teachers

There are many different kinds of English student, for example:

- those for whom English is their first language and is spoken at home
- those who are taught in English at school, but speak another language with their family at home
- those who are bilingual and attend schools where some lessons are conducted in English and others in another language
- those who attend international schools where many languages are spoken, but all lessons are conducted in English
- those who join a school later with less fluent English than their peers who have been at the school longer.

Whatever the situation, this presents challenges for English teachers because their students' use of English will vary according to whether it is a language that they use for leisure or simply for learning. This will lead to huge variations in vocabulary, the ability to adapt language for informal and formal situations and the 'natural fluency' of your students' writing. This challenge is addressed in more detail in Chapter 10 **Inclusive education** and Chapter 9 **Language awareness**.

Teacher Tip

Ensure that you are aware of your individual students' strengths and weaknesses in spoken English and use this knowledge to focus on specific skill development in your lessons. For many students using speaking and listening activities can help build their confidence and develop their fluency.

Another challenge facing English teachers is the place of English in the curriculum as a core subject. The fact that students have not chosen the subject can make it seem like a chore, or something that they are being forced to study. Luckily, the majority of students realise that English is an important global language so will take the subject seriously, but they may be more concerned with its functional use and find the more literary and analytical aspects of the subject superfluous to their perceived needs. As an English teacher, you have to inspire them to appreciate the richness of the language and the opportunities that it opens up in terms of reading great works of literature, or being able to talk about complex and important topics with ease.

Resources for English teachers

English teachers rarely rely solely on textbooks to cover a course for them, but they do contain some useful materials for individual lessons. To keep lessons interesting, students sometimes need to be surprised! Look out for articles, passages or powerful images in newspapers and magazines that you can use to stimulate discussion and exploration in the classroom. This will ensure that you are always using new resources that students will connect with real-life experiences.

Resource sharing is a crucial part of any English department and many departments have a member of staff responsible for collating and organising pooled resources. This is a great way of ensuring not only that less experienced teachers are able to access tried and tested resources, but also that more experienced teachers try out new ideas and different approaches to their teaching. If your department doesn't share resources, you could be the person to change that!

Teacher Tip

As mentioned above, the most important resource in the English classroom is you! If you keep abreast of developments in technology and current pedagogical thinking through focused CPD, your own planning and research and resource sharing across your department, you will be able to plan a challenging and lively curriculum and your students will thrive.

Challenges faced by students studying First Language English

The three main areas of assessment are Reading, Writing and Speaking and Listening. Within these areas there are specific challenges for learners.

Reading

When responding to unseen texts on an examination paper, students have to apply advance reading skills such as skimming and scanning to select relevant material, reading for meaning (both explicit and implicit), understanding perspective and modifying material for directed writing and analysing the writer's use of language for specific effects. Students need to develop independent reading skills and understand the different question types that they might face.

You cannot rely on teaching reading skills through the study of literary texts only. The range of reading offered in lessons needs to be as wide as possible to broaden the students' experiences of different text types. It should include:

- literary texts
- informative texts
- persuasive texts
- media texts
- biography and autobiography
- travel literature.

Writing

Learners might need to write in different styles and for different purposes in both Reading and Writing examinations. These may include:

- informative writing
- discursive writing
- narrative writing
- descriptive writing
- personal writing.

Many students will find some writing styles more challenging than others. It is crucial that you achieve a balance between allowing students to express themselves freely and develop their own writing styles, and insisting on accuracy in spelling, punctuation and grammar. Remember that when you are asking your students to write, they are creating, which is at the top of the revised Bloom's taxonomy of skills (Figure 4.1).

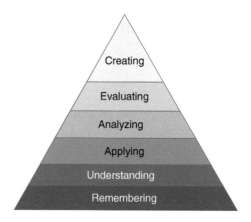

Figure 4.1: Bloom's Taxonomy – Revised.

Many learners are less confident about descriptive and narrative writing. Unlike the creative subjects (Drama, Art, Dance or Music), teachers of English do not have specialist teaching areas designed to support the creative process. Learners in English will often be asked to write a creative short story sitting at their desk in a classroom. It is essential that when asking students to become writers, an appropriate atmosphere is created. This could involve changing the seating arrangements, working away from the classroom or playing a piece of music to stimulate creativity. It is also essential that when you look at students' first attempt at the opening of their story, you resist the temptation to point out errors, but instead focus on the power of the writing and its effect on the reader.

Speaking and Listening

Many students are more confident when expressing their ideas orally in lessons, often because their oral skills are more developed than their writing skills. However, some are nervous when they have to do more formal presentations, especially the Speaking and Listening assessments.

Offering your students opportunities to demonstrate their understanding through speaking is essential in a First Language English course. The ability to do presentations, interviews, group discussions and role-plays is an essential skill for the working world and also allows you to test students' understanding of a text or topic without having to set written work. It also encourages careful listening and engenders a respectful working environment in the classroom, where everyone has the right to express their views and be listened to. Offering plenty of opportunities in speaking and listening will develop your students' thinking skills, their vocabulary, their confidence and their reasoning.

LESSON IDEA 4.1: DEVELOPING CONTENT KNOWLEDGE

This lesson idea explores a discursive topic: 'Are we becoming too dependent on technology at the expense of real communication?'

You can integrate the development of reading, writing and oracy skills through the planning and preparation of any discursive writing task. This lesson idea focuses on developing the students' content knowledge and understanding of the topic through research (reading articles and websites), oracy (delivering a presentation to the class on the topic) and writing (drafting and writing a discursive essay).

Lesson 1: Students are given articles to read and make notes from (summary skills). They can also research online.

Lesson 2: Students prepare a presentation to deliver to the class in pairs or groups (oracy skills).

Lesson 3: Students draft write a discursive essay (writing skills).

Summary

Chapter 4 has focused on the challenges facing teachers and learners in First Language English. Ask yourself the following questions:

- What are the most important lessons you have learnt since becoming an English teacher?

- How much does what you learn on CPD courses affect your classroom practice?

- How do you approach creative writing with your students?

- How much do you use speaking and listening to develop your students' skills in English?

Interpreting a syllabus

5

What is a syllabus?

A syllabus provides a framework of what we should teach over a given time period, usually one or two years. The syllabus may be provided by an examination board, or by your education ministry. In this chapter we will consider what is contained in a typical English syllabus and how you should use it to support and plan your teaching. The syllabus may be published in hard copy, but is also usually available online and can be printed out. A syllabus contains vital information to allow you to plan your teaching programme to ensure that you cover all the requirements and prepare your students fully for any assessed work or examinations.

These are the key areas of the syllabus that you will need to familiarise yourself with before you can plan your programme of study:

1 The learning objectives

The learning objectives state the overall aims of the syllabus: what students need to achieve to succeed. Examples may include:

- to enable candidates to understand and respond to what they hear, read and experience
- to enable candidates to communicate accurately, appropriately, confidently and effectively
- to encourage candidates to enjoy and appreciate a variety of language.

The learning objectives will not tell you what to teach, but you need to ensure that what you are teaching addresses them.

2 The assessment components

You will need to look carefully at the assessment components outlined in the syllabus. Some courses offer different options and routes. There may be two different tiers of the same examination paper, where students can be entered either for an extended-tier or a core-tier paper. You may also be able to do a coursework component instead of an examination paper.

Some courses offer a Speaking and Listening component as a separately endorsed assessment. This is usually optional.

A description of each component will be included in the syllabus. The description will explain how an examination paper will be divided into different sections and the types of question that will be asked in each section. It will also explain how many marks are allocated to each section and question, as well as how each component addresses the different assessment objectives. Many English syllabuses have different papers for assessing the Reading and Writing assessment objectives, although some questions may address them both.

3 The content

English is a skills-based subject, therefore you will find that there is very little specific content in an English syllabus. You can base your understanding of the content on what is outlined in the assessment objectives as they will guide your teaching of the skills that are needed to succeed. In the English classroom the teaching of reading and writing skills is usually integrated, as students study the work of successful writers and are influenced to use the techniques and qualities of the reading texts they study in their own writing.

4 Assessment objectives

The assessment objectives for First Language English are divided into the three areas for assessment: Reading, Writing, and Speaking and Listening. The objectives will explain what skills are being assessed in each area. For example, Reading assessment objectives may include understanding implicit meanings, or analysing how writers achieve effects, whereas Writing assessment objectives will include using a range of vocabulary effectively, or sequencing facts, ideas and opinions coherently. You will notice that there are direct links between what students should achieve in their own writing, and the features that they analyse in what they read. Therefore, although the assessment objectives are divided into Reading and Writing, the teaching of the skills required can be approached holistically.

Teacher Tip

Note that the assessment objectives for Speaking and Listening usually overlap with those for Reading and Writing – this is intentional to allow you to build in speaking and listening activities to support and enhance your lessons through the whole course.

Planning your teaching

Planning a programme of study is essential to ensure that you deliver the syllabus fully and prepare your students for all the assessment components. However, the essential part of planning your teaching is to ensure that you are not constrained by the syllabus. English teachers are free to design their own curriculum, using topics and texts that they think will interest their students, as well as introducing them to key concepts, skills and themes. Focusing on examination technique early in the course will not be helpful in ensuring that students are developing the wider skills needed to develop their reading and writing. Building the students' confidence to take risks and experiment with ideas and techniques is far more important to make their learning successful and enjoyable.

Teacher Tip

When examination boards publish assessment objectives, they establish a clear understanding between themselves and teachers as to what is to be tested. They are not trying to tell you what you should teach!

Structuring and scaffolding learning

If you are teaching English Language skills alongside English Literature, you can use the set texts being studied to develop the reading and writing skills needed for English Language. Many of you will teach First Language English as a separate subject, but you are still likely to use reading texts as a key resource.

It is important to build reading skills gradually, rather than expecting students to tackle past papers at the beginning of the course. A student cannot begin to answer questions on writers' craft until they can answer questions about explicit and implicit meanings. Asking students to do questions that are too challenging can simply dent their confidence and give them a negative attitude towards the subject. It is more advisable to start with easier reading texts and focus on developing their independent reading skills by giving them more accessible tasks that test their overall understanding of vocabulary in its contextual use. When you feel confident that they are ready to explore the inferred meanings in texts, or identify bias, you can begin to introduce them to more challenging material.

In English, skills need to be layered; unlike many subjects the curriculum in English cannot be divided into chunks of content to be learnt before students move on to the next topic. Each term students will add another layer to their understanding and skills, through reading more complex material and developing their vocabulary and writing skills to use more complex language and structures in their own writing. Think of it as a spiral, as illustrated in Figure 5.1.

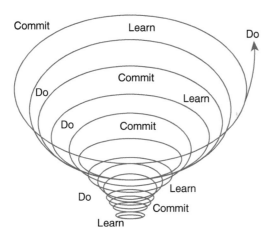

Figure 5.1: The upward spiral.

Teacher Tip

You may like to consider the relative difficulty of the different reading skills that learners need, and find texts where just one skill can be focused on. Look at the following list and decide whether you agree with the order the reading skills are in:

- scanning
- skimming
- explicit meaning
- implicit meaning
- selecting quotations
- identifying techniques
- questioning
- fact and opinion
- bias
- inference
- analysing language and structure.

At which point in the course would you introduce these reading skills?

In writing, asking students to produce openings to stories and descriptive writing can be an excellent way of encouraging them to think carefully about every word and sentence and its impact on the reader. Rather than expecting learners to produce whole compositions, asking them to produce shorter pieces that focus on exploring one particular skill or technique can be a more effective way of teaching writing skills. See Chapter 6 **Active learning** for lesson ideas on developing narrative and descriptive writing skills.

Some teachers favour a thematic approach to the teaching of English. This can involve the study of literature and developing writing and reading skills while exploring a topic or theme over the course of a half term. Themes such as conflict, love, places or technological advances can be explored through a range of fiction and non-fiction texts, poetry, articles and other resources. Students can develop their own writing in a range of styles and explore the topic through debates and discussions. A thematic approach to the teaching of English is explored in more detail in Chapter 12 **Global thinking**.

Summary

Chapter 5 has considered how you may plan a programme of study to prepare students to meet the assessment objectives for a First Language English course. Look back over the material presented and consider the following:

- How do you plan your programme of study to ensure that individual skills are developed carefully?

- Have you considered a thematic approach to your programme of study?

- How can you use past papers as a useful resource, rather than let them drive your teaching?

6 | Active learning

What is active learning?

Active learning is a pedagogical practice that places student learning at its centre. It focuses on *how* students learn, not just on *what* they learn. We as teachers need to encourage students to 'think hard', rather than passively receive information. Active learning encourages students to take responsibility for their learning and supports them in becoming independent and confident learners in school and beyond.

Research shows us that it is not possible to transmit understanding to students by simply telling them what they need to know. Instead, we need to make sure that we challenge students' thinking and support them in building their own understanding. Active learning encourages more complex thought processes, such as evaluating, analysing and synthesising, which foster a greater number of neural connections in the brain. While some students may be able to create their own meaning from information received passively, others will not. Active learning enables all students to build knowledge and understanding in response to the opportunities we provide.

Why adopt an active learning approach?

We can enrich all areas of the curriculum, at all stages, by embedding an active learning approach.

In active learning, we need to think not only about the content but also about the process. It gives students greater involvement and control over their learning. This encourages all students to stay focused on their learning, which will often give them greater enthusiasm for their studies. Active learning is intellectually stimulating and taking this approach encourages a level of academic discussion with our students that we, as teachers, can also enjoy. Healthy discussion means that students are engaging with us as a partner in their learning.

Students will better be able to revise for examinations in the sense that revision really is 're-vision' of the ideas that they already understand.

Active learning develops students' analytical skills, supporting them to be better problem solvers and more effective in their application of knowledge. They will be prepared to deal with challenging and unexpected situations. As a result, students are more confident in continuing to learn once they have left school and are better equipped for the transition to higher education and the workplace.

What are the challenges of incorporating active learning?

When people start thinking about putting active learning into practice, they often make the mistake of thinking more about the activity they want to design than about the learning. The most important thing is to put the student and the learning at the centre of our planning. A task can be quite simple but still get the student to think critically and independently. Sometimes a complicated task does not actually help to develop the students' thinking or understanding at all. We need to consider carefully what we want our students to learn or understand and then shape the task to activate this learning.

Why use active learning in English lessons?

As a subject which focuses on skill development, English lends itself to active learning in the classroom. Active learning encourages students to make connections between concepts, ask themselves meaningful questions and then search for answers. To do this, they need to be provided with active learning opportunities which shift the focus from teacher instruction to student engagement. For example, many of your students may be passive readers who find it challenging to interact with and annotate texts. Modelling your own active reading of a text, to show them how to sharpen their thinking through making connections and asking themselves pertinent questions, can help students to see that knowledge needs to be constructed carefully, rather than expecting easy answers.

How can English teachers establish a classroom where active learning can take place?

- By creating a positive learning environment.
- By encouraging intellectual curiosity.
- By encouraging students to take risks.
- By developing resilient students.
- By giving students opportunities to reflect on their learning.
- By planning lessons through thinking about skills as well as content.

In an active learning classroom the teacher is the most important resource, and it is crucial that you play an active role in each lesson, guiding your students through carefully planned activities that are designed to offer opportunities to collaborate, build up knowledge and skills, and, most importantly, develop their abilities to think and make reasoned judgements. All of the lesson ideas in this chapter demonstrate how you can do this through a range of activities designed to develop descriptive, discursive and narrative writing skills.

Effective methods of establishing active learning in the English classroom

Collaborative learning

Learning collaboratively has many advantages for students: it allows discussion, peer feedback, reflection and improvement. It can also encourage students to develop a more creative approach to their own learning, accepting that failure is sometimes a more crucial tool in the process of learning than immediate success. When students produce work collaboratively, they are more likely to make judgements about their learning throughout the process, instead of producing a finished piece of work and relying on teacher feedback to improve their next piece. This means that that feedback becomes part of the process of learning. This is explored in more detail in Chapter 7 **Assessment for Learning**.

Teacher Tip

When putting students into pairs or groups, think carefully about balancing abilities, skills and personalities to ensure the best learning processes and outcomes.

▣ LESSON IDEA ONLINE 6.1: COLLABORATIVE WRITING

Many students find descriptive writing challenging. This lesson idea involves a whole class writing a description collaboratively. Each group of four is only asked to write one sentence inspired by an image, which encourages them to think very carefully about each word they write. The sentences are then arranged to form an opening paragraph, with the class collaborating to decide in which order the sentences are most effective.

Visible Thinking

Visible Thinking is a framework or routine that is used to facilitate the accomplishment of a specific task. It offers students opportunities to make their thought processes visible through inviting them to externalise their thoughts and express them in spoken or written forms.

Visible Thinking integrates the process of students' thinking with content learning and encourages a creative mindset which is eager to take up learning opportunities. Using Visible Thinking routines guides students' thought processes and encourages active thinking.

In the English classroom it is common for students to react to ideas too quickly, offering unsubstantiated viewpoints and assertions; Visible Thinking routines actively encourage a measured and thoughtful process of thinking by slowing down responses and ensuring that thoughts and questions are based on what has been carefully observed. It also stimulates curiosity and inculcates a culture of inquiry in the classroom. This is an essential skill in English when students are responding to unseen texts and have to show perceptive understanding through close reading. Many read the texts too quickly and make judgements immediately, instead of adopting a slower process of thinking by recognising the different layers of meaning within the text. Starting by using Visible Thinking routines through the use of images, allows the development of transferable skills that will encourage much closer reading of texts.

One of my favourite activities is the See, Think, Wonder thinking routine from the Visible Thinking programme at Harvard University – Project Zero. Through this routine, teachers can promote the development of a student's thinking; students are encouraged to be 'thinking rich' and it becomes part of the classroom culture very quickly. The routine is particularly useful in the English classroom, where students need to develop analytical and discursive skills backed up by evidence and a clearly developed thought process.

In this routine, the teacher puts an image on the whiteboard and asks the learners to follow this process:

- SEE – what do you see? Describe the picture.
- THINK – what do you think about when you look at the picture?
- WONDER – what does this picture make you wonder?

This works well as a collaborative activity where students share their ideas. They should also be encouraged to write down their observations under the headings, SEE, THINK, WONDER. This will allow them to trace their earlier thought processes. One of the challenges that you will face as a teacher is that many students will try to jump to THINK too quickly, or may not even recognise the difference between SEE and THINK, or the difference between THINK and WONDER. Encouraging them to slow down and follow the steps is a key role of the teacher in this process. By spending time describing what they can see, and focusing on minute detail in the image, they will open up many more opportunities for THINK (what questions the picture makes them ask) and WONDER (what wider thoughts and questions the picture stimulates).

☑ **LESSON IDEA ONLINE 6.2: VISIBLE THINKING ROUTINE**

This lesson idea uses See, Think, Wonder to introduce a topic for discursive writing. Rather than introducing a given topic, this lesson allows the learners to decide the topic as they undertake a Visible Thinking routine.

Teacher Tip

Try using this Visible Thinking routine with a piece of text or an unseen poem.

For more information and ideas on Visible Thinking routines search for 'The Harvard Project, Visible Thinking'.

Encouraging active reading

In English examinations, students are required to respond to unseen reading passages. Many will skim-read the passage to find the answers to comprehension questions, which can lead to a superficial understanding of the passage. This affects their ability to respond to questions which require inference. Encourage students to read passages more carefully to develop an overview of the meaning and the writer's intentions.

LESSON IDEA 6.3: UNSEEN PASSAGES

A Visible Thinking routine can be used when looking at unseen passages and texts:

Stage 1: What is the passage about?

Stage 2: What is the purpose of the passage – the writer's intentions?

Stage 3: How does the writer use language to achieve that purpose?

Working collaboratively can make this more effective, as students share ideas and understanding:

- Split the class into two sets of three groups.
- Give each of the groups a different passage – A, B or C. (These can be any passages you choose.)
- The passages should be pasted onto a large piece of paper.

For the first activity the groups read their passage and write notes for stage 1 – what is this passage about?

Then swap the passages around the three groups. Each group should read the first group's notes on stage 1 and add to them if necessary before doing stage 2 – what is the purpose of the passage, the writer's intentions?

Finally, the passages should be rotated again and the groups should read and add to the first two groups' notes before doing stage 3 – how does the writer use language to achieve that purpose?

Teacher Tip

When putting students into groups, you can give each student a specific responsibility: the strongest reader could read the passage aloud to the group, a second student could write the notes, another student could highlight the passage for stage 3.

Slow writing

Slow writing is a process that encourages students to think carefully about how they construct a narrative, sentence by sentence. Students should use double-line spacing so that they can go back and redraft their writing. It means that they will think about each word they write and what will make their writing effective for the reader.

In the introduction to slow writing, it is useful if you model an example you display on the whiteboard (for instance Figure 6.1) with a clear set of instructions for writing the opening of a piece of narrative writing based on the image.

Figure 6.1

- Your first sentence must start with an adverb.
- Your second sentence must contain only three words.
- Your third sentence must contain a semi-colon.
- Your fourth sentence must be a rhetorical question.
- Your fifth sentence will start with an -ing word.
- Your sixth sentence will contain a simile or metaphor.

When they have finished, display the teacher's modelled response on the board:

> **Sadly**, I put my arm around his shoulder, pulling him close to me. **It was terrible.** Mother and father were **gone; they** couldn't look after us now. **How could they do this to us, to their children? Trembling**, I told him that I was his big brother. I would be **a lion standing guard over him**.

You can then ask the class (in groups) to write the next paragraph using these instructions:

- Your first sentence will be only one word.
- Your second sentence will contain a colour.
- Your third sentence will use direct speech.
- Your fourth sentence will use alliteration.
- Your fifth sentence will begin with an adverb.
- Your sixth sentence will contain a twist.

Teacher Tip

The instructions can be altered to suit the ability range of the students and to reflect what they have been learning. A good extension activity is to ask the groups to devise instructions for paragraph 3 themselves.

Using questions to activate learning

To be successful active learners, students need to develop intellectual curiosity: they must want to know more. Using questioning effectively as their teacher will help them achieve this, as it will also teach them to question effectively.

To do this you should model and encourage:

- questions on different levels: questions that open up wider implications
- asking more abstract or philosophical questions
- asking reflective questions to reinforce own understanding.

The Socratic method of questioning

Applying a system of questioning with a clear framework is a great way of making your students more aware of effective questioning. For example, following the Socratic method of questioning, outlined in the bullet points below, can work in any number of classroom situations. Putting the Socratic method on the whiteboard and modelling its use is an effective way of developing students' understanding.

Remind students to:

- clarify
- challenge assumptions
- probe for evidence and reasons
- consider different viewpoints and perspectives
- consider implications and consequences
- question the question.

Here is an example of how you could model the use of the Socratic method of questioning in a lesson where students are discussing a discursive writing topic about inequality:

- **Clarify:** what did you mean when you said that people make their own luck in life?
- **Challenge assumptions:** does that mean that you think people who are poor always deserve to be poor, or are there sometimes circumstances that they can't control?
- **Probe for evidence and reasons:** what examples can you give that show that people always get what they deserve?
- **Consider different viewpoints and perspectives:** do you think that other people may argue that sometimes people are born with advantages that others don't have?
- **Consider implications and consequences:** what do you think about someone who makes money through crime, or wins a fortune on the lottery?
- **Question the question:** do you still think that people always make their own luck in life?

Encouraging abstract thinking

Thunks

Thunks are questions that have no right or wrong answer, but are designed to make students think! They encourage abstract thinking about everyday things, which stimulates students' curiosity about the world around them. They make excellent starters to lessons where you want learners to engage in active learning.

For example:

- If you were a day of the week, which day would you be?
- If you do a good deed because you were forced to, have you still done a good deed?

Reflection

Building in time for students to reflect on their own learning is essential in active learning. Students should consider how they have contributed to collaborative work, how they have built on prior knowledge to construct effective learning, and identify areas for improvement. Ways in which you can encourage your students to be more reflective are considered in Chapter 7 **Assessment for Learning**.

Flipping the classroom

You are probably used to teaching using the traditional model of a classroom, one where the teacher is the central focus, imparting knowledge and giving instructions to the students in lessons, then setting tasks for homework that require the students to demonstrate their understanding and application of what has been learnt. Although this is clearly effective practice, in a 'flipped classroom' the learning environment is reversed and teachers deliver the content knowledge needed through online methods, using lesson-time for the activities and tasks that would usually be set for homework. The content knowledge may be delivered through online videos prepared or sourced by the teacher, or students may be required to undertake reading and research at home. The advantage of a 'flipped classroom' is that it allows more time in the classroom to be spent on the construction of knowledge through focusing on higher-order thinking skills such as problem-solving. It also allows students to work collaboratively when applying their knowledge to activities set by the teacher, resulting in a less didactic and more active learning environment.

There is a misconception that flipped learning can only work in Mathematics, Science and similar subjects where problem-solving is part of the learning process, but it can work in all subjects where there is content to consume at the students' own pace, and class time can be used to review and apply the learning. Figure 6.2 (Williams, Beth, 2013) uses Bloom's Taxonomy to explain how the 'flipped classroom' allows class time to be used to develop higher-order skills, where the students have the advantage of their teacher's presence.

When teaching extended writing, many teachers use lessons to prepare students for the topic and plan their writing, whereas in a 'flipped classroom' the students would research and plan at home and use lessons to explore the process of writing.

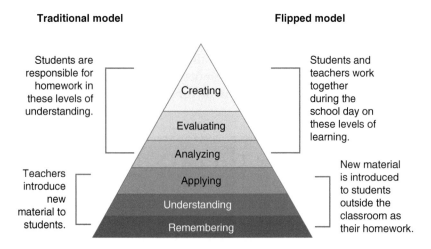

Figure 6.2: Bloom's Taxonomy in the 'flipped classroom'.

Teacher Tip

At this point you may like to ask yourself the following questions about using active learning approaches in your classroom:

- How would you need to adapt your classroom?
- How would you need to adapt your teaching style?
- How would you need to adapt your lesson planning?

Potential obstacles to active learning

Many teachers worry about how their lessons will be perceived in an active learning English classroom, especially as lessons where active learning is taking place are unlikely to be silent. The important thing to remember is that in lessons where classes are sitting and working individually in silence, their greatest resource – you as their teacher – is not being used!

It is important that your classroom is organised to maximise active learning efficiently. Think about the layout of your tables; you want to be able to lead and facilitate learning, so it is important that you have an area of the classroom where you can be seen easily by the whole class – this does not have to mean standing at the front, in fact it may mean standing in the middle of the classroom!

You may also need to consider a sign that will tell your class that you want them to listen to you. Many teachers have a signal such as standing in a particular position in the classroom and raising their hand when they want silence.

It is also important that the students learn to listen to one another respectfully, and again, this is something that will need to be developed. It is likely that you will want groups of students to feed back to the whole class about what they have been learning, and you will need to develop your own systems to ensure that they can do this effectively. It is important that their enthusiasm for the activity they are undertaking does not prevent them from listening to each other and to you.

Teacher Tip

It is important to remember that in an active learning classroom:

- the teacher has to take a step back and allow students to take charge of their learning
- the teacher needs to scaffold tasks carefully to ensure that learning is focused and that each stage of the activity is carefully constructed

- students need self-discipline, which is developed through strong guidance
- trust must be established in the classroom, so that all students are prepared to take risks.

Summary

Chapter 6 has focused on effective ways in which active learning activities can be used in the English classroom. Look back over the material presented and reflect on the following questions:

- When you plan your lessons, do you consider the learning skills being developed as well as the content being taught?

- How can you adapt your lessons to make students think more deeply?

- Do you build in time for your students to reflect on their learning?

Assessment for Learning

7

What is Assessment for Learning?

Assessment for Learning (AfL) is a teaching approach that generates feedback that can be used to improve students' performance. Students become more involved in the learning process and, from this, gain confidence in what they are expected to learn and to what standard. We as teachers gain insights into a student's level of understanding of a particular concept or topic, which helps to inform how we support their progression.

We need to understand the meaning and method of giving purposeful feedback to optimise learning. Feedback can be informal, such as oral comments to help students think through problems, or formal, such as the use of rubrics to help clarify and scaffold learning and assessment objectives.

Why use Assessment for Learning?

By following well-designed approaches to AfL, we can understand better how our students are learning and use this to plan what we will do next with a class or individual students (see Figure 7.1). We can help our students to see what they are aiming for and to understand what they need to do to get there. AfL makes learning visible; it helps students understand more accurately the nature of the material they are learning and themselves as learners. The quality of interactions and feedback between students and teachers becomes critical to the learning process.

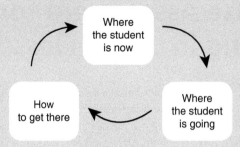

Figure 7.1: How can we use this plan to help our students?

We can use AfL to help our students focus on specific elements of their learning and to take greater responsibility for how they might move forward. AfL creates a valuable connection between assessment and learning activities, as the clarification of objectives will have a direct impact on how we devise teaching and learning strategies. AfL techniques can support students in becoming more confident in what they are learning, reflective in how they are learning, more likely to try out new approaches, and more engaged in what they are being asked to learn.

What are the challenges of incorporating AfL?

The use of AfL does not mean that we need to test students more frequently. It would be easy to just increase the amount of summative assessment and use this formatively as a regular method of helping us decide what to do next in our teaching. We can judge how much learning has taken place through ways other than testing, including, above all, communicating with our students in a variety of ways and getting to know them better as individuals.

Why use Assessment for Learning in English lessons?

In this chapter we will consider how we can use Assessment for Learning (AfL) in the English classroom through adopting different teaching techniques and using a range of activities and tools in our lessons.

In English lessons, a student's ability in reading and writing has to be carefully aligned to ensure that what they are reading is appropriate and helpful to the development of their writing skills. It is also crucial that there is an emphasis on the development of oracy skills to encourage natural fluency in their writing. You can create opportunities for formative assessment with students who are learning English by establishing a classroom in which dialogic teaching flourishes. This means giving students time to rehearse and practise, and to listen to teachers and to peers modelling and scaffolding language. Students should be given opportunities to think and talk collaboratively, before producing language themselves.

How can we assess understanding?

AfL does not mean testing students more regularly or setting them more written exercises for you to mark. It means developing an awareness of their progress and understanding, and offering them feedback that can be applied to improve their learning. We have to move beyond asking our students whether they understand so that we can move on to the next topic. Instead, we should ensure that we ask the right questions to accurately assess students' understanding so that they can move on themselves. This is when assessment *of* learning becomes assessment *for* learning.

LESSON IDEA 7.1: EXPLAINING METAPHOR

Think about a lesson where you have introduced the concept of metaphor. Consider whether you assessed the students' understanding of how to use a metaphor effectively, rather than their understanding of what a metaphor is.

If you asked them to copy down your examples of metaphors then make up their own examples, how effectively did that test their understanding? Could they have just modelled their examples on yours?

Try this lesson idea as a more effective way to test students' understanding of how metaphors work.

Suggest a metaphor that you think describes you as a teacher – a conductor of an orchestra, or a gardener, for example. Write your metaphor up on the whiteboard and talk to the class about why that metaphor is appropriate for you. In your explanation, extend the metaphor. For example, if you have chosen a gardener, you may tell them that you think of the class as the flowers and shrubs that you have planted, and your lessons and activities as the water and nourishment that they need to grow as learners. Explain that a gardener has to be patient and work tirelessly to see their garden bloom at the right time.

Ask each member of the class to think of a metaphor to describe themselves as a student. Ask them to write their metaphor on a sticky note and swap with their neighbour. They should explain their metaphor to their neighbour in the same way that you explained yours to them. Then you can pick some students to introduce their partner to the class through explaining the metaphor that they chose. Some of the metaphors may be humorous, some may be honest and moving, but they will all tell you whether that student understands how to use a metaphor meaningfully.

Assessing the skills of analysis and evaluation

Analysis and evaluation of reading passages require higher-order thinking skills, which can be challenging for students to develop and challenging for teachers to assess. Often, students read passages superficially, skimming through them to find answers to comprehension questions. Although this can enable them to answer questions testing explicit understanding of individual words, phrases or sentences, it often leads to confusion in questions where they have to adopt a more analytical approach or evaluate information through selection and synthesis, or by adopting a different perspective in their own writing.

One way of developing the skills necessary for analysis and evaluation is by encouraging students to read unseen passages more carefully to form an overview of the text's purpose, style, tone, language and structure. Lesson idea 7.2 uses collaborative questioning to develop an understanding of a range of unseen passages. It encourages deeper reading and the ability to link analysis of language and structure to an overview of the writer's intentions.

☑ LESSON IDEA ONLINE 7.2: PASSAGES

During this activity, that takes place over two lessons, groups of students rotate around five tables, each with a different unseen passage. Each group has eight minutes to read the passage and work through a series of stages, each building on the work of the previous group. In the second lesson each group presents one reading passage to the rest of the class, offering an overview of the text's purpose, style, tone, language and structure.

Setting clear targets for learning

Students need to understand what they are learning and why they are studying. Many teachers put lesson objectives on the whiteboard at the start of the lesson to ensure that students are clear about the aims of the lesson. However, there is evidence that suggests that simply putting up objectives is not enough to ensure that students are really clear about what you are trying to achieve. You need to talk to them and contextualise the aims of the lesson within the wider scheme of work or unit of study. An effective way of doing this can be to produce the aims of the lesson in conjunction with the students in the class. You should also refer back to the aims during the lesson to keep them relevant and revisit them in a plenary to allow students to reflect on whether they have achieved the objective.

Teacher Tip

Try asking your class to work out the aims and objectives at the end of a lesson. This can be a great way of finding out whether the lesson has achieved what you intended it to.

Using effective questioning

Quick questioning to monitor understanding

Using questioning effectively in the classroom is more complex than most people appreciate. If we ask a question and allow students to raise their hands, do we assume that those who don't raise their hands don't know the answer? Or, do we assume that all those who raised their hands do know the answer? If a student answers correctly, could it be a lucky guess? Could it just be the students who have been listening carefully raising their hands? Could it be that the less confident students automatically don't raise their hands? Could it just be the quickest students who raise their hands whereas the more reflective ones want to think about the answer more carefully? However we answer those questions, it is clear that simply asking a question and asking students to raise their hands has limitations in terms of assessing understanding across a class.

However, sometimes we do want to ask a whole class a quick question to ensure that a concept has been understood. There are many tools used by teachers to improve this type of questioning and make it more effective:

- Some teachers have a bag of sticks, each with an individual student's name on it. They pick a stick to offer the answer.
- Use of individual whiteboards is popular. Each student writes down their answer and holds the board up when requested.

- There are electronic versions of the above where students can use tablets or smart phones to type in a response. The teacher can immediately see who has selected the correct answer.

Wait time

Research shows that most of us don't wait long enough before seeking an answer to a question. If we allow the class some time for thought and processing, a larger number of students will offer a response to our questions. This is crucial for students who process information more slowly or for more reflective students. When asking a question of the whole class, tell them that you are going to allow them a minute before responding, but make it clear that you expect an answer at the end of that time. This will improve the quality of the answers you receive.

Closed and open questions

Closed questions – those that require a yes or no answer, or can be answered with a fact – do have their place in the English classroom, but when you want to elicit more detailed and thoughtful responses, questions need to be more open. English students have to develop skills of analysis, evaluation and synthesis, so use of open questions is essential to make them consider the deeper meanings of texts. For example, when studying an extract from *Of Mice and Men* you may ask the class whether Curley's wife is the only woman on the ranch, to which the correct answer would be 'yes'. A more open question would lead to development of greater understanding, for example 'How does Curley's wife's position as the only woman on the ranch affect the way that she is treated?'

Think-Pair-Share

This technique works very well with open questions like the example from *Of Mice and Men*. Each student should think individually before sharing their ideas with a partner or small group. Their ideas should be discussed and consolidated before they share them with the rest of the class. How much time is given will depend on the complexity of the question.

☑ **LESSON IDEA ONLINE 7.3: THINK-PAIR-SHARE**
This idea incorporates the concept of Think-Pair-Share in a group
discussion, preparing students for a piece of discursive writing.

Pose, Pause, Pounce, Bounce

This is a simple but effective strategy to encourage students to actively
think and question. It requires you to design an effective question which
you *pose* to the class. You then *pause* to allow the students to absorb the
question and think carefully about their response. You then *pounce* on
one student for their response and *bounce* it to another student. This
allows the class to build on one another's ideas and encourages active
participation in class.

Teacher Tip

Discuss what makes a good question with your students. The
process can make them explicitly understand the difference
between open and closed questions. They can write their
own questions on a given topic in pairs and try them out on
another pair.

Feedback

Assessing learning allows us to give clear feedback to our students,
both positive feedback and constructive advice on how they can
improve further.

Traditionally, many students and teachers have defined feedback as a
written comment and grade at the end of a marked piece of work, or
verbal feedback from a teacher following a presentation or contribution
to a lesson. Many students are only interested in the grade that is given
for a piece of work and therefore often fail to recognise that the grade
is meaningless unless they have absorbed the feedback given to explain
how the grade was awarded, and how the work could have been

improved. There is a strong argument for not using grades or marks on pieces of work being used for formative assessment to ensure that the student focuses on the feedback rather than the grade. You may find that your students are resistant to this idea, but if carefully explained, they should recognise that it is far more conducive to effective learning.

There is a school of thought which argues that teachers spend far too much time marking written work. As an English teacher you are likely to spend hours each week carefully annotating written work. How often do you get the impression that you are repeating the same feedback on several students' work, or even repeating feedback that you have given individual students before, sometimes many times? Some teachers believe that rather than mark each individual piece of work, you should read them all making careful notes, then offer feedback to the whole class, going through common weaknesses and misconceptions, as well as highlighting good practice. You can refer to individual pieces, read some sections aloud and encourage full discussion and questioning. This is far less time-consuming than marking individual pieces of work and is likely to promote much more discussion of the learning process, with students actively involved in their own learning.

The best feedback involves the student directly and encourages them to take responsibility for their own learning; rather than assuming that feedback should always come from teacher to student, think about ways in which students can give feedback to one another, or give feedback to you as their teacher on their own learning. This results in a dialogue being formed between the teacher and learner, which is far more likely to result in the learner moving forward with clear targets and goals for improvement.

Formative assessment – how it works

Figure 7.1 demonstrates the hierarchical principles underpinning successful formative assessment and makes it clear that the responsibility for effective formative assessment lies with the teacher. You must show students what is expected by determining exactly what they need to do and know. It is only at that point that peer and self-assessment can take place successfully.

Teacher Tip

Teach collaboration! Peer assessment requires students to work collaboratively. Discuss collaboration with your students and ask them to identify the skills needed to collaborate successfully. In groups, ask them to write each skill on a sticky note and create a Diamond 9 (see Figure 7.2), where they place the skills in order of importance. Ask the groups to present their Diamond 9s to the rest of the class.

After they have completed this exercise, ask them to reflect and give feedback on how they used collaborative skills to create their Diamond 9.

Figure 7.2: A Diamond 9.

Tools for peer feedback

Try using some of the following tools for peer feedback. As illustrated in Figure 7.1, it is essential that before students undertake peer assessment they must fully understand the learning objectives and what the intended outcomes of the work are.

- Peer marking – students mark one another's work and offer feedback.
- Students produce their own mark schemes – they work collaboratively to decide how learning outcomes can be measured through marking.
- Student corrections – they are asked to correct one another's work.
- Thoughtful dialogue – students are offered a framework to share ideas. The teacher establishes a set of principles for discussion, such as everyone contributing and listening before responding.

- Shared self-reflection – this could be through discussion, or through reading one another's reflection journals and responding to them.
- Talk partners – this encourages more reluctant speakers to share views and ideas with another student.

▣ LESSON IDEA ONLINE 7.4: PEER REVIEW

This idea demonstrates how peer review can work when students draft openings for creative stories. Students read one another's openings and are given a sheet to devise constructive feedback for discussion.

Reflection

To ensure that your students reflect on their learning, you need to be a reflective practitioner yourself and model that to your class. One way of encouraging a reflective approach to learning is to get your students to think about what they have learnt and identify where there may be room for improvement.

At the beginning of a lesson, you can start by reflecting on how well the previous lesson went, using feedback from the students as well as your own observations. You can explain any areas that you may wish to go back over with the class, or how you plan to consolidate their understanding in future lessons. The important thing here is flexibility and making your students aware that your lesson will build on previous knowledge and understanding. This allows you to create a supportive working environment, something that is essential for Assessment for Learning to take place.

You can use a variety of methods to get feedback from your students, including plenary discussions, reflective journals, giving starters to reflective statements or group discussions where students consider their own learning.

Teacher Tip

Some teachers encourage students to fill in a sticky note and place it on a message wall as they leave a lesson. The messages can indicate where students feel secure or areas where they would like more consolidation. The teacher can use these messages to plan and adapt the next lesson. This encourages reflection in the students and ensures that the teacher offers an open dialogue with them.

Summary

In Chapter 7 we have considered how to make Assessment for Learning work for you and your students in English Language lessons. Ask yourself the following questions:

1 How reflective are you and how do you encourage your students to be reflective learners?

2 How carefully do you think about your use of questioning?

3 How much of your feedback is dependent on written comments on marked work? Would you be able to spend less time but give more useful feedback if you followed the suggestions in this chapter?

4 Have you encouraged the development of the collaborative skills your students need to work together to support one another's learning?

5 How do you ensure that the learning process is a dialogue between you and your students?

8 | Metacognition

What is metacognition?

Metacognition describes the processes involved when students plan, monitor, evaluate and make changes to their own learning behaviours. These processes help students to think about their own learning more explicitly and ensure that they are able to meet a learning goal that they have identified themselves or that we, as teachers, have set.

Metacognitive learners recognise what they find easy or difficult. They understand the demands of a particular learning task and are able to identify different approaches they could use to tackle a problem. Metacognitive learners are also able to make adjustments to their learning as they monitor their progress towards a particular learning goal.

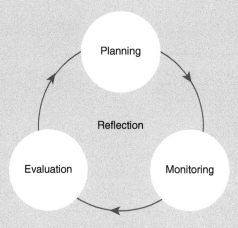

Figure 8.1: A helpful way to think about the phases involved in metacognition.

During the *planning* phase, students think about the explicit learning goal we have set and what we are asking them to do. As teachers, we need to make clear to students what success looks like in any given task before they embark on it. Students build on their prior knowledge, reflect on strategies they have used before and consider how they will approach the new task.

As students put their plan into action, they are constantly *monitoring* the progress they are making towards their learning goal. If the strategies they had decided to use are not working, they may decide to try something different.

Once they have completed the task, students determine how successful the strategy they used was in helping them to achieve their learning goal. During this *evaluation* phase, students think about what went well and what didn't go as well to help them decide what they could do differently next time. They may also think about what other types of problems they could solve using the same strategy.

Reflection is a fundamental part of the plan–monitor–evaluate process and there are various ways in which we can support our students to reflect on their learning process. In order to apply a metacognitive approach, students need access to a set of strategies that they can use and a classroom environment that encourages them to explore and develop their metacognitive skills.

Why teach metacognitive skills?

Research evidence suggests that the use of metacognitive skills plays an important role in successful learning. Metacognitive practices help students to monitor their own progress and take control of their learning. Metacognitive learners think about and learn from their mistakes and modify their learning strategies accordingly. Students who use metacognitive techniques find it improves their academic achievement across subjects, as it helps them transfer what they have learnt from one context to another context, or from a previous task to a new task.

What are the challenges of developing students' metacognitive skills?

For metacognition to be commonplace in the classroom, we need to encourage students to take time to think about and learn from their mistakes. Many students are afraid to make mistakes, meaning that they are less likely to take risks, explore new ways of thinking or tackle unfamiliar problems. We as teachers are instrumental in shaping the culture of learning in a classroom. For metacognitive practices to thrive, students need to feel confident enough to make mistakes, to discuss their mistakes and ultimately to view them as valuable, and often necessary, learning opportunities.

Using metacognitive processes in the English classroom

One of the most important aspects of a teacher's role is teaching our students how to learn. As English teachers, we are teaching a subject which is concerned with the development of skills rather than the acquisition of knowledge; it is crucial that we stimulate intellectual curiosity in our students, challenging them to become active, rather than passive, learners. For some students this is their natural approach to learning, but for most it has to be nurtured and developed through teaching methods that deliberately seek to empower them and create independent thinking. As students grow older, they develop a larger repertoire of learning strategies, but it takes time to model how to use new strategies when they are younger. Much of the information in this chapter will directly link to the theory and lesson ideas explored in the chapters on active learning and Assessment for Learning, developing the concept of self-regulated learners. This term refers to learning that is guided by metacognitive processes such as planning, monitoring and evaluating personal progress. Self-regulated learners are successful because they take control of their learning environment.

Metacognitive processes also include memory, attention, activation of prior knowledge and using cognitive strategies to complete a task or solve a problem. These are processes that lend themselves to English and they can be built in to a wide range of learning activities in the English classroom.

Transferable skills

As English teachers, we have to teach students to recognise that many of the skills that they learn are transferable. A student who learns to analyse poetry skillfully often fails to transfer the analytical skills that they apply to poetry when given a non-fiction article to read. Many of our students are willing to take texts at face-value without using metacognitive processes to ask themselves why a writer has phrased something in a certain way and what their overall intention may be. Metacognitive process will encourage deeper thinking when reading texts and allow students to access the meanings of texts more successfully.

Teacher Tip

Teaching English students to become aware of the methods and processes that they are applying as they read different texts will enable them to apply those processes and methods to other areas of their reading and writing, thus enabling them to build upon their learning experiences and become better learners.

Scaffolding and modelling

Metacognition demands careful input by the teacher in the form of scaffolding and modelling. We have to scaffold the process of metacognition until the student is at a point where we can stand back, remove the scaffolding and be confident that the structure will stay firmly in place. To model it, we must make it clear that we use metacognitive processes ourselves and demonstrate it through thinking aloud as we teach. More detail on this kind of modelling will come later in this chapter.

Self-awareness

To be self-aware in their learning, students need to recognise their strengths and weaknesses. We identified the importance of feedback in Chapter 7 **Assessment for Learning**, as well as how important it is for students to reflect on their learning to become better learners. One of the key features of self-awareness is a student understanding how they think and process information most efficiently. For some, this may require a silent library, whereas others may need a noisier environment or background music. It may be that the ideal learning environment changes according to the subject they are studying, or the skill they are developing. The important thing is that students recognise their own ideal learning environment.

In English, self-awareness is also crucial for successful exploration of thoughts and feelings and to develop empathy with others. In their writing and reading tasks, students are constantly exposed to the perspectives of others and need to understand their own position relative to the world around them. Developing awareness of how their own experiences have shaped them, and how others may have different experiences leading to a different set of beliefs or values, is crucial to developing the empathy and imagination necessary to successfully evaluate and interpret texts, or to develop as writers who can move beyond viewing everything from their own perspective.

The self-regulated learning cycle in practice

The self-regulated learning cycle (see Figure 8.1 at the start of this chapter) outlines the phases involved in metacognition as explained in the introduction to this chapter. Let's look at how each of these phases may work in an English lesson where you have set the students the task of creating an effective opening to a narrative story. The learning objective for the lesson is to use a variety of sentence structures for specific effect.

Planning

The planning phase indicates that students need to understand the learning objectives of any lesson and what they are being asked to do. Within the learning objectives, students may set their own goals to complete the task successfully.

So, if the task is to create an effective opening to a narrative story, and the learning objective is to use a variety of sentence structures for specific effect, you will need to provide a learning framework to enable the students to consider:

- their prior knowledge of different sentence types, including how to construct complex sentences using a variety of punctuation, how to use short sentences for deliberate impact and how to vary the beginnings of sentences for effect

- past experience they have of using different sentences for effect, both in their own writing and in what they have read
- past experience of strategies for planning writing.

They may also consider their own learning goals at this point. For one student, that may be to work more attentively without distractions, for another it may be to avoid overuse of the semi-colon. The important thing is that each learner sets themselves individual short-term learning goals for the task.

Monitoring

In this phase, the students will monitor what progress is being made towards their learning goal. Through monitoring they will determine whether they are managing to achieve the success criteria, or whether they need to adopt a different learning strategy. If students do not have a large repertoire of learning strategies at their disposal, you will need to provide appropriate amounts of scaffolding to help them practise.

In this lesson example (to create an effective opening to a narrative story), as the students begin to develop their writing they should be continually monitoring their progress by measuring the effectiveness of their writing and trying out different ideas. This could involve some peer review and feedback with students reading one another's writing and offering constructive feedback. This would need to be carefully planned so that students' feedback is specifically guided towards areas of improvement, for example use of particular language or imagery. Students should also be encouraged to seek help and advice during this stage, as self-regulation does not mean that they should try to accomplish each task alone, but should seek help and advice from others with the goal of making themselves a more autonomous learner. A student may try making changes to their writing as a result of this feedback, perhaps by changing the types and order of sentences to gain maximum effect. Throughout this process they should be adapting and changing their writing.

Evaluation

This is the phase where the students consider how successful the strategies used to develop the task were. When they have completed the task and written their opening to a narrative story, they evaluate the success of their work. They consider what they may do differently next time and whether they could use different strategies to make their writing better. They may also think about whether the planning methods they used could be useful for other aspects of their work.

Teacher Tip

Students are more likely to become successful self-regulated learners when they are able to evaluate their own learning without a teacher's summative assessment. Some students will show you a rough draft of their writing and ask you what grade it would get, and it is important that you do not offer summative feedback during this process. Instead, the student should be encouraged to consider their own learning goals and how successful the strategies they adopted were.

Reflection

As you will see, throughout the phases of planning, monitoring and evaluation, reflection is a fundamental part of each process. Through reflection, students are continually aware of the learning process and taking control of their learning.

Reflection is something that also needs to be scaffolded and modelled by the teacher. There are many students who resist looking back and reflecting on their working processes, just wanting to move on to the next piece (where they will often make the same errors or display the same weaknesses). You will need to cite examples of how reflection helps you as a teacher, for example, modelling your own reflections of the lesson to your class, thus demonstrating how you may adapt your teaching strategies next time.

Teacher Tip

Giving your students a clear system for reflection, such as a reflective worksheet or a reflection journal, will help them develop reflective habits.

⊡ LESSON IDEA ONLINE 8.1: USING THE SELF-REGULATED LEARNING CYCLE

A series of three lessons which focus on effective structuring of discursive writing using the self-regulated learning cycle. Students consider the question: Is it preferable to live in a town or a city? They are encouraged to consider alternative ways of structuring and developing an argument as well as using research effectively.

Useful tools for encouraging metacognition

Learning journals

A successful way of helping students to monitor their own thinking is through using personal learning journals. These can take the form of a series of questions which students answer. The questions should focus on *how* they learnt rather than *what* they learnt. These are some questions that they may find useful:

- What learning did I find easy this week, and why?
- What learning did I find the most challenging, and why?
- What planning and monitoring strategies did I find most helpful?
- What will I try to improve upon next week and how will I do this?

Thinking aloud

This is a process where the student thinks aloud while completing a task. Although not always practical in a classroom setting, it enables students to actively experience how they are thinking as they learn, which promotes self-awareness of the learning process. It is something that you can model for them to demonstrate the process, then explain that they can think in their head as they try it themselves.

LESSON IDEA 8.2: DESCRIBING THOUGHTS

This lesson idea offers you an effective way of modelling thinking aloud by looking at an example of a directed writing question from a past examination paper. You could use any directed writing question for this lesson.

> Recently, an elderly relative of yours fell awkwardly when she was shopping and suffered minor injuries. A young person helped her and then left the scene immediately afterwards. Your relative is very grateful to the young person, and asks you to write a letter to the local newspaper to thank and praise the young person.
>
> Write your **letter**. You must include the following:
>
> - the date **and** details of how the accident happened
> - what injuries she suffered **and** what the young person did to help
> - why it is important to let people know about this incident.
>
> Cover all three points above **in detail**.
>
> You should make sure your letter is polite and informative. Start your letter 'Dear Editor', and remember to add an appropriate ending.
>
> *Cambridge International O Level English Language 1123, Paper 12, task 1, June 2015*

You can describe your thoughts as you read the question and think carefully about the requirements.

'I'm going to start by considering the style, purpose and audience of my directed writing. I can see that it's about an elderly relative of mine, so I'll assume that I'm a young person and the relative is my grandmother. It's definitely a female relative because it says 'her'.

'The style is a letter and the audience is a newspaper editor, so it's a formal letter. That's an interesting audience because although I'm writing to the editor, my letter would be published, so I need to consider that it's an open letter. It's a local newspaper, so it could be read by my friends, neighbours and teachers as well as people that I don't know. That will affect the tone of my writing.

→

'The purpose is to thank the young person who helped my grandmother. Oh, hang on ... I also have to praise him or her. It doesn't say what gender the young person was, so I'll have to decide that too. I suppose the purpose is really to make everyone aware that there are good young people around, who help people with no desire for praise.

'Now, I need to look closely at the bullet points, to make sure I think really carefully about the details I include. I have to make sure that I develop them all as fully as I can ...'

And so on.

This lesson is a good method of demonstrating the amount of thought that needs to be applied when faced with a question of this complexity in an examination. Students often miss the finer detail and clues in the question.

▣ LESSON IDEA ONLINE 8.3: THINKING ALOUD

Based on another directed writing task, this lesson idea encourages your students to think aloud as they plan their response. This lesson follows on from your modelling of thinking aloud.

Exam wrappers

An exam wrapper is an activity that is based on an examination paper and integrates a metacognitive process. It involves a short intervention that encourages students to look beyond the grade or mark awarded. An exam wrapper usually involves the student considering three questions:

1 How did I prepare for the exam?
2 What kind of errors did I make on the exam?
3 What could I do differently next time?

This strategy is not just suitable for exams: the same questions could be used as a wrapper after any piece of completed work.

Question 1: How did I prepare for the exam? requires students to reflect on how they prepared for an exam or a piece of work, which necessitates them having to reflect on the choices they made about their learning. See Figure 8.2.

Figure 8.2

When a student sees a grade on an exam paper or on a piece of work, they often find it difficult to move beyond it. This can mean that they don't think carefully enough about their performance in the exam. **Question 2: What kind of errors did I make on the exam?** is designed to make students analyse their work in more depth, leading to constructive feedback. See Figure 8.3.

Figure 8.3

When responding to **Question 3: What could I do differently next time?**, students should use their responses to the first and second questions to think about how they should approach the next exam or piece of work. This question aims to help students to make connections between their study choices and the work produced so they can predict what learning strategies will be more effective in the future. Students should look back at their responses to the first two questions then list specific ways they might prepare differently next time to improve their performance. See Figure 8.4.

Figure 8.4

☑ LESSON IDEA ONLINE 8.4: EXAM WRAPPER

This lesson idea explores how to use a wrapper in a summary activity to improve selection, synthesis and use of own words.

Summary

In Chapter 8 we have explored how you can encourage metacognition in your English lessons to create more self-regulated learners who take responsibility for their own learning.

- Metacognition is effective for learners of all abilities but needs to be taught.

- Students need to know what the learning objective(s) and success criteria are so that they can plan how to approach a task.

- You need to model strategies that students can use to plan, monitor, evaluate and reflect on how they are learning.

- Make time in your lessons for students to practise becoming more self-regulated learners.

- Make time for student reflection and offer appropriate strategies.

- You need to model thinking aloud to help your students develop this process.

9 | Language awareness

What is language awareness?

For many students, English is an additional language. It might be their second or perhaps their third language. Depending on the school context, students might be learning all or just some of their subjects through English.

For all students, regardless of whether they are learning through their first language or an additional language, language is a vehicle for learning. It is through language that students access the learning intentions of the lesson and communicate their ideas. It is our responsibility as teachers to ensure that language doesn't present a barrier to learning.

One way to achieve this is to support our colleagues in becoming more language-aware. Language awareness is sensitivity to, and an understanding of, the language demands of our subject and the role these demands play in learning. A language-aware teacher plans strategies and scaffolds the appropriate support to help students overcome these language demands.

Why is it important for teachers of other subjects to be language-aware?

Many teachers are surprised when they receive a piece of written work that suggests a student who has no difficulties in everyday communication has had problems understanding the lesson. Issues arise when teachers assume that students who have attained a high degree of fluency and accuracy in everyday social English therefore have a corresponding level of academic language proficiency. Whether English is a student's first language or an additional language, students need time and the appropriate support to become proficient in academic language. This is the language that they are mostly exposed to in school and will be required to reproduce themselves. It will also scaffold their ability to access higher order thinking skills and improve levels of attainment.

What are the challenges of language awareness?

Many teachers of non-language subjects worry that there is no time to factor language support into their lessons, or that language is something they know little about. Some teachers may think that language support is not their role. However, we need to work with these teachers to create inclusive classrooms where all students can access the curriculum and where barriers to learning are reduced as much as possible. An increased awareness of the language needs of students aims to reduce any obstacles that learning through an additional language might present.

This doesn't mean that all teachers need to know the names of grammatical structures or need to be able to use the appropriate linguistic labels. What it does mean is that we all need to understand the challenges our students face, including their language level, and plan some strategies to help them overcome these challenges. These strategies do not need to take a lot of additional time and should eventually become integral to our process of planning, teaching and reflecting on our practice. We may need to support other teachers so that they are clear about the vocabulary and language that is specific to their subject, and how to teach, reinforce and develop it.

The importance of language awareness in the English classroom

For many of your students, English may not be the language spoken in their homes. This can pose many challenges for teachers of First Language English because assessments expect natural fluency in English, which requires students to adapt their language to different situations, both informal and formal. They will also need to develop the academic language necessary to analyse and evaluate texts, using appropriate subject terminology accurately and effectively.

You may also have a wide variety of English proficiency in your classroom, where some students are very fluent English speakers, but others are still struggling with using grammatical constructions accurately in their oral and written work. Some students may be more developed in spoken English, but find it challenging to express their ideas in extended writing. It is common for students to learn vocabulary then use it awkwardly or imprecisely in written work because they have not learnt to use it naturally. Some students learn lists of idioms, but when they include them in their compositions they sound unconvincing or contrived, or they overuse them in a way that a native English speaker would not.

This chapter will consider how best you can support your students in developing their language skills and developing language awareness by offering support and scaffolding to develop natural fluency.

Teacher Tip

You may find the following useful when considering your own language in the classroom:

- supporting clear verbal instructions with written instructions on the whiteboard
- ensuring that you use appropriate subject terminology accurately, particularly when using command words

- modelling language use for students – getting students to repeat language back to you can be very effective.

The importance of developing oracy skills

Improving written language is dependent on developing high levels of oracy skills in the classroom. We can do this through offering ample opportunities for speaking and listening activities, which can be linked to written assignments. It is crucial that we teach our students to use academic English in their oral communication, as this has a huge impact on their ability to write in academic English. Students who can articulate their thoughts confidently and fluently when speaking are more able to do the same in their written work.

Using spoken language in the classroom is essential to helping build up fluency and confidence in using language appropriately for different purposes. Many teachers find that they can support their students' development of oracy by using the following support tools:

- an oracy framework to measure progression in spoken language skills—this framework should consider linguistic, cognitive and physical skills (see Figure 9.1, an oracy framework devised for a Cambridge research project)
- creating speaking frameworks, to help students scaffold their extended talks and presentations
- creating discussion guidelines to ensure that discussion is focused
- creating discussion roles to structure language effectively for different purposes
- using role-play to teach students to adapt their spoken language in different contexts.

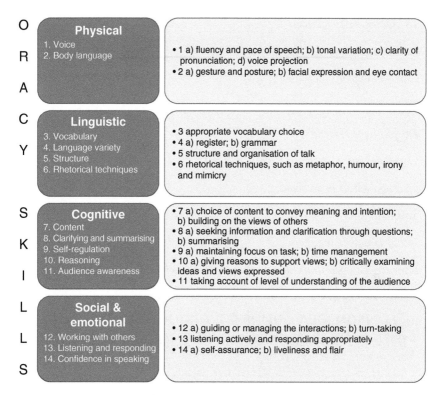

Figure 9.1: An oracy skills framework.

To develop effective skills in speaking and listening, the role of the teacher is crucial in setting appropriate tasks that will support students' learning as part of a wider curriculum, and offer appropriate scaffolded tasks to enable them to develop skills in a variety of roles. For example, when doing group discussions, you can help structure the activity by giving students different roles within the group, such as the initiator, the clarifier, the prober or the challenger. This will make students think carefully about the spoken contributions that they make.

To scaffold the language that they use, you can use sentence starters to help them recognise different types of contributions to discussion.

To initiate a discussion:

Let us start by …

To begin our discussion we need …

Today we are going to be discussing …

To ask for clarification:

Can you give us an example of …

Can you explain more about …

To probe:

Do you have evidence …

Can you justify what you have said about …

Can you tell us more about …

To challenge:

If that is true, how …

I can see why you think that, but have you thought …

☑ LESSON IDEA ONLINE 9.1: GROUP DISCUSSIONS

This lesson idea explores effective language use in a group discussion on school topics.

Helping students to build up the language needed for directed writing tasks

When a student looks at a directed writing question, they are being asked to show considerable understanding of language use, both in reading the question, and in considering the language choices they make when writing their response.

Look at the following directed writing task where key words have been highlighted:

> The manager of a large hotel wants to employ full-time members of staff such as receptionists or chefs. The manager wishes to hire and train students who are about to leave school. You decide to write a letter to the manager to apply for one of the jobs.
>
> Write your **letter**. You must include the following:
>
> - which job you are applying for **and** why you would like to do this work
> - details of your achievements in and out of school and why they make you suitable for the post
> - how you would like to develop your career in the hotel business.
>
> Cover all three points above **in detail**. You should make your letter polite and informative.
>
> Start your letter 'Dear Sir / Madam', and remember to provide a suitable ending.
>
> *Cambridge International O Level English Language 1123, Paper 11, task 1, November 2013*

Think about what understanding of language a student reading this question needs, and how, as a teacher, we can support our students in these language demands:

1   The task – a formal letter applying for a job.
2   Language considerations – the language of the workplace. The question contains terms such as *large hotel, manager, receptionist, chef* and *hire and train*. This makes several assumptions about the student's grasp of the language for a situation that is likely to be outside their own experience. It will require them to use vocabulary and written expressions suitable for language of the workplace.
3   The tone – students should recognise that this is a formal letter and that the language they use should be formal and polite. They are also required to choose which job they are applying for, explain why and to consider their suitability for the post and their wider career development. This is a particular type of communication where they have to present themselves in a positive light without being arrogant or gushing.
4   The structure – students will need to consider the structure of their letter carefully. The bullet points will help them, but they will also

need to consider how they reveal information about themselves and make their opening and endings effective.

Now look at another directed writing task, where key words have also been highlighted:

Imagine that your aunt and uncle are considering educating your cousin at home and have asked for your views. Your cousin is an only child and, in your opinion, rather spoilt.

Write a letter to your aunt and uncle in which you should explain:

- the advantages of being home schooled
- the reasons why home schooling may not be advisable
- why you would or would not recommend home schooling for your cousin.

Be careful to use your own words.

Address each of the three bullets. Begin your letter: 'Dear Aunt and Uncle ...'.

Cambridge IGCSE First Language English 0500, Specimen Paper 3, Q1, November 2013

Think about what understanding of language use a student reading this directed writing question needs and how we can develop the language they need to access the tasks:

1   The task – an informal letter to the writer's aunt and uncle. Note that although this is not a formal letter, the student has to consider that a letter to an aunt and uncle is not as informal as a letter to a friend. The difference in age and the relationship to an aunt and uncle would imply that a degree of formality is required through being polite and respectful, yet warm and friendly. They would also need to think about how they may appropriately sign off a letter to relatives.

2   Language considerations – the language here is mixed. The question contains terms such as *educating* and *home schooled*, which will allow the student to use their own experience to a certain extent. The language in the question also makes it clear that the student is being asked to express views and offer advice.

3   The tone – students should recognise that the language they use should be polite and friendly. Although in the question it says that

they consider their cousin to be spoilt, students need to consider whether they would express this in a letter to the child's parents, or whether they would need to adapt the language to be tactful and diplomatic.

4   The structure – students will need to consider the structure of their letter carefully. The bullet points will help them, but they will also need to consider how they balance the different viewpoints, offer sound advice and make their opening and endings effective.

As directed writing tasks can require students to write a letter, speech, report or article, and can involve situations of varying formality, students need a pre-prepared body of language to tap into in order to access these tasks. In Chapter 12 **Global thinking**, there are more suggestions of how you can develop these writing styles through topic-based teaching.

Ways to support students' language development

Role-play

There are many reasons for incorporating role-play into English lessons. Role-play allows students to explore different people's situations and perspectives through putting themselves in an imaginary situation for a specific speaking activity. To prepare your students for directed writing tasks in particular, using role-play is an effective way of building up their vocabulary for different scenarios as well as adopting appropriate vocabulary for a range of different voices. Making role-play an integral part of your English curriculum will enable your students to explore language and develop their skills while adding variety and pace to lessons.

You can use role-play to explore a variety of situations where students are required to use functional language. Examples of useful scenarios are job interviews, eating out, travelling and formal committee meetings. Many of these relate to scenarios used for directed writing tasks and will enable students to think quickly about how language needs to be adapted for different situations and voices. Through role-play you can broaden your classroom to include real-life situations, thus offering a much wider range of language opportunities.

Role-play activities require students to find new language. This can be done by exploring the vocabulary needed before the activities start, or the teacher can be used as a 'floating dictionary' as they monitor the activities and feed in new language as the need arises. As the students develop they should become more autonomous and use dictionaries to look up new vocabulary themselves.

Developing language through role-play allows students to acquire new vocabulary and constructions in a natural environment. It is crucial to building up the natural fluency required for first language syllabuses, particularly when writing about situations that may be unfamiliar to their everyday lives.

Teacher Tip

Using role-play can be an excellent way of exploring language in different contexts and for different purposes. It allows students to build up and use vocabulary that will help them with directed writing tasks.

☑ LESSON IDEA ONLINE 9.2: ROLE-PLAY

This lesson idea outlines the use of role-play to explore language in different contexts and helps students adapt their language to reflect different levels of formality. It uses situations from directed writing tasks to explore role-play.

Command words in questions

In reading questions, students need to be aware of the different requirements of command words in the question stem, such as *give*, *describe*, *suggest*, *explain*, *support*, *analyse* and *evaluate*. Students need to be able to differentiate between these command words to answer questions correctly.

Advising students to circle or underline command words is good practice, but students also need to be clear about their meanings.

Teacher Tip

Make sure your students are aware that command words often indicate the kind of response required. The command word *give* for example, will often indicate a single word or phrase, whereas the command word *explain* will often require a more developed answer in their own words.

Developing vocabulary

Helping students develop and widen their vocabulary is an intrinsic part of English teaching. For a student to express themselves clearly and effectively, they need to develop a vocabulary that allows them to express nuance and different shades of meaning. They also need to use the correct vocabulary for different writing styles they are expected to adopt in directed writing tasks and compositions. We have already looked at how using discussions and role-play can help to broaden a student's vocabulary and will now consider other strategies:

- Plan the introduction of new vocabulary which relates to texts or topics being studied.
- Have a 'word of the lesson' displayed in your classroom and model its use at several points in the lesson. Attempt to use it in context as many times as possible.
- Model specific writing strategies to develop vocabulary, for example drawing on synonyms or word families linked to meaning and intensity.
- Explore prediction of story through the use of reading passages.
- Pre-teach vocabulary before meeting it in a text, for example key words such as technical terms, or words in unfamiliar contexts.
- Check understanding of vocabulary meaning through targeted questioning, particularly in guided reading and writing sessions.
- Model a piece of writing in front of the class, verbally explaining vocabulary choices as you write.
- Use guided writing sessions to support small, targeted groups to review a piece of writing and challenge vocabulary choices made.
- Use peer review to discuss vocabulary choices in writing.
- Provide a range of quality texts and text types that link to and extend the students' interests.
- Create interactive wall displays so that students can capture new and unusual vocabulary for later use.

(Adapted from Teaching Effective Vocabulary, Department for Children Schools and Families, 2008.)

Working with other departments

As an English teacher, how do you support other departments in your school to ensure that students develop language awareness in content-driven subjects? There is much that can be done to make sure that the English department offers appropriate support for the development of language skills across the whole school.

Ask yourself the following questions:

1   How much do I know about what my students are studying in other classes where the curriculum is content driven?
2   How could I support the teachers of those classes in ensuring that students develop the language needed to access the content?
3   Do I have information about the language abilities of students that other teachers could find useful?

To work more closely across school departments to integrate content and English Language classes, you should consider the following:

- Observing lessons across different departments to see what goes on in different classrooms. You could make notes on the language demands of content lessons and how they could be supported by the English department.
- How you could support the development of different language skills needed for content lessons, such as reading questions.
- How resources are used in content lessons – could classroom wallcharts, worksheets, textbooks or ICT resources be used more helpfully to support language development?
- Asking students about areas of difficulty and/or challenge in other subjects.
- Supporting other departments' long-term planning by integrating the needs of content subjects in the English curriculum. Developing academic language through the skills of essay-writing, note-taking, summarising and evaluating can all be supported through the teaching of English.
- Doing some team-teaching with other departments to enable content and language teachers to work together. The content teacher can focus on concepts and the English teacher can focus on language.

- Linking language lessons to the content being studied in another subject. For example, when studying grammatical structures, use the content of a topic being studied in History lessons.

☑ LESSON IDEA ONLINE 9.3: BRINGING CONTENT INTO THE ENGLISH LANGUAGE CLASSROOM

This lesson idea explores how you could teach language structures using a history topic, the French Revolution.

Summary

In Chapter 9 we have considered how to become more language aware in our teaching of English.

Remember the following points:

- developing skills in oracy will have an enormous impact on your students' fluency and confidence when writing

- students need to be taught specific subject terminology

- there are lots of ways to extend your students' vocabulary

- as an English teacher, you can support your students in their language development across the curriculum

- as an English teacher you can support your colleagues delivering content curriculum.

10 | Inclusive education

What is inclusive education?

Individual differences among students will always exist; our challenge as teachers is to see these not as problems to be fixed but as opportunities to enrich and make learning accessible for all. Inclusion is an effort to make sure all students receive whatever specially designed instruction and support they need to succeed as learners.

An inclusive teacher welcomes all students and finds ways to accept and accommodate each individual student. An inclusive teacher identifies existing barriers that limit access to learning, then finds solutions and strategies to remove or reduce those barriers. Some barriers to inclusion are visible; others are hidden or difficult to recognise.

Barriers to inclusion might be the lack of educational resources available for teachers or an inflexible curriculum that does not take into account the learning differences that exist among all learners, across all ages. We also need to encourage students to understand each others' barriers, or this itself may become a barrier to learning.

Students may experience challenges because of any one or a combination of the following:

- behavioural and social skill difficulties
- communication or language disabilities
- concentration difficulties
- conflict in the home or that caused by political situations or national emergency
- executive functions, such as difficulties in understanding, planning and organising
- hearing impairments, acquired congenitally or through illness or injury
- literacy and language difficulties
- numeracy difficulties
- physical or neurological impairments, which may or may not be visible
- visual impairments, ranging from mild to severe.

We should be careful, however, not to label a student and create further barriers in so doing, particularly if we ourselves are not qualified to make a diagnosis. Each child is unique but it is our management of their learning environment that will decide the extent of the barrier and the need for it to be a factor. We need to be aware of a child's readiness to learn and their readiness for school.

Why is inclusive education important?

Teachers need to find ways to welcome all students and organise their teaching so that each student gets a learning experience that makes engagement and success possible. We should create a good match between what we teach and how we teach it, and what the student needs and is capable of. We need not only to ensure access but also make sure each student receives the support and individual attention that result in meaningful learning.

What are the challenges of an inclusive classroom?

Some students may have unexpected barriers. Those who consistently do well in class may not perform in exams, or those who are strong at writing may be weaker when speaking. Those who are considered to be the brightest students may also have barriers to learning. Some students may be working extra hard to compensate for barriers they prefer to keep hidden; some students may suddenly reveal limitations in their ability to learn, using the techniques they have been taught. We need to be aware of all corners of our classroom, be open and put ourselves in our students' shoes.

Is your classroom inclusive?

The majority of teachers differentiate, both as a natural aspect of their approach to their teaching, and also because they know their students well and treat them as individuals. But as always, with teachers there is a nagging suspicion that we can do more, and many teachers find themselves asking the question, is my classroom truly inclusive? We all need to respond to different learning needs and this requires us to make adjustments to our teaching for all levels of ability, as well as considering the difficulties faced by learners with specific educational needs.

There are lots of things that we can consider as English teachers who want to ensure that our classroom is truly inclusive regardless of the needs or difficulties of each individual student.

For example, most teachers will automatically:

- give individual feedback on a student's work
- vary class questioning
- provide a range of resources
- praise
- work with selected groups or individuals
- do pair and group work
- assess understanding through a mix of oral and written response
- vary tasks
- allow students to explore personal interests
- allow students a choice of reading material
- encourage students to ask questions.

All of the above indicate good classroom practice that, if done effectively, will lead to inclusive learning where all students feel equally valued.

Teacher Tip

Use the list above as a checklist. Are there any other practices that you undertake to ensure inclusivity in your English classroom?

Knowing your students

When students arrive in your class, they do so as individuals, and if they are a new student, they may have varying experiences of English teaching in their previous schools. It is important to quickly grasp their skill levels through setting them a piece of writing, listening to them read and observing their discussion and presentational skills. In English lessons this can be done quickly by starting the year with a collaborative activity incorporating a range of tasks.

Whether you are teaching English to classes that are 'streamed', where a student's class is decided by their ability level assessed through previous performance or formative assessments, or you are teaching a mixed-ability class where the ability levels of your students vary dramatically, you will still need to differentiate between your students' needs and approaches to learning to ensure that every student can access the learning in each lesson and achieve their full potential.

A wide-ranging understanding of each of your students' abilities across the different skills needed for successful outcomes in English examinations is crucial to ensure that you can offer differentiated learning in your classroom. You may know an individual student's reading and writing abilities through reading tests, prior examination performance and a range of baseline data available to you, but you also need to know their particular weaknesses and difficulties so that you can devise teaching and learning strategies to help them. For example, if you have a student who finds it challenging to decode complex words when reading independently, you may use phonics to help them recognise similarities in the sounds made by groups of letters. You could also ask such students to keep a reading log of how they solved problems in decoding while reading. They could also record the strategy they used to approach the word, and how it worked. These logs will help students think about which strategies were most successful so they can use them again in more independent situations. This works well for older readers; other students may lack confidence about reading aloud, and ensuring that you hear them read regularly, but not in front of the whole class, will help. Knowing your students well maximises your power to help them achieve their potential.

Some of your students may have been diagnosed with a particular learning difficulty, for example dyslexia or slow processing skills. If they have had a learning profile created, it will offer you guidance and advice on how best to approach specific elements of the English curriculum. Other students' challenges may be less definable or explicable, but they may still need higher levels of support to enable them to access the full content of your lessons.

Teacher Tip

Where a student in your class has been granted extra time in assessments due to the diagnosis of a specific learning difficulty, you will need to offer guidance on how they should best utilise that time. Do not assume that they will automatically adjust the timings spent on each task themselves; they will need support and encouragement to use the time wisely.

Think about the following:

1   What is your school's provision for learners with special educational needs? Are you fully aware of the support available to them (and you!)?
2   What information do you need to know and how can you access it? Are there members of staff who can support you?
3   What would you need to do if you suspected that one of your learners may have a special educational need?

Teacher Tip

Hopefully, you know your students well and any diagnosed special educational needs will be considered carefully when planning lessons, but there are some issues that may not be permanent, or are undiagnosed, such as emotional or social difficulties. These issues could affect whether an individual student can access the learning in each lesson. It is important that you are always observant and respond when you suspect that one of your students is not accessing the learning being offered.

Thinking about your language

As English teachers, we spend a great deal of time talking to our students. We talk to them for a variety of reasons and purposes: to explain a task; to teach a concept; to comment on their work; to ask them questions to test their understanding; to remind them of their responsibilities … the list is endless. But how do we know that the student we are addressing has fully understood our expectations? This is an even bigger consideration when we are addressing a whole class where there could be a wide range of issues affecting communication, such as language comprehension abilities, physical disabilities, concentration issues, behavioural problems or mental health issues.

Differentiated instruction

It is crucial that we offer all students equal access to learning content. This means that all students must understand what they are being asked to do and what the learning outcome should be. This can be achieved by explaining a task or activity in different ways. You can use the whiteboard to project a slide of step-by-step instructions, while explaining it verbally using different language. You can explain it more than once, altering your language as you clarify what you want the learners to do.

Another effective approach is to adapt tasks for different learners to enable them all to achieve the best outcomes. For example, you may divide a discursive composition question into different components for some students who find extended responses difficult because they find it challenging to structure their answers. Giving them three bullet points to scaffold their response allows them to plan carefully, and can ensure that they address all of the assessment objectives.

Differentiated support

Different students need different levels of support to get to the same place in their learning. It is not always practical to give completely different reading resources and tasks to different students, particularly when you want to work with a whole class. Using differentiated worksheets that are based on the same reading material, but offer different routes to prepare students for the main task, can be an effective way of offering extra support for the students that need it, while at the same time ensuring that they are still working at a level appropriate for the syllabus being studied.

☑ LESSON IDEA ONLINE 10.1: ANALYSIS OF A PASSAGE

This demonstrates how tasks can be carefully scaffolded to lead students to a more extended question on an unseen fiction passage. For students who need more support with independent reading, the shorter questions on Worksheet 1 ensure that their exploration of the passage is carefully scaffolded, beginning with a synopsis of the passage, then guiding them to particular lines to explore language use. Worksheet 2 is adapted for higher ability students, where there are still some scaffolded tasks, but they are expected to do more selection and offer greater analysis. Eventually, both worksheets lead all learners to the same task for assessment.

Teacher Tip

When teaching composition writing, you will find that some students require a greater level of support to help them structure their writing effectively. Using writing plans can help students develop the skills to structure their writing more effectively, and the level of support offered can be slowly reduced as the students' own skills develop further.

Remember that students with emotional or social difficulties may find creative writing challenging. You should always offer choices of topics and be aware that some students will use these tasks as a way of exploring complex personal challenges. You may be able to utilise these tasks to support these students.

☑ LESSON IDEA ONLINE 10.2: PLANNING NARRATIVE WRITING

This lesson idea focuses on teaching composition writing using a narrative writing plan. This encourages students to think about various aspects of what makes a narrative composition effective for the reader. It is helpful for students who find narrative writing challenging.

How you arrange your classroom

Hopefully, your classroom is arranged with the students in groups to encourage discussion and active learning. If you prefer your learners to sit in paired tables, ensure that they can be moved together easily when there is an opportunity for group work.

If students are sitting in groups, you can organise them to ensure that they can support one another. Many teachers prefer to sit their students in groups arranged by ability, others prefer to have mixed-ability groups, where the stronger students can support the ones who need more help. You don't have to have one set of groups – you can have a number of different seating arrangements according to the nature of the activity you are doing! Moving students around allows you to differentiate and also gives them opportunities to work with different peers at different times.

Groups could be arranged according to the following criteria:

1   By ability — sitting students of similar abilities together can allow you to differentiate and use appropriate stimulus materials. For example, if the students were looking at a reading passage, each group could have a different reading passage and question types or discussion points pertinent to their ability level. This can allow you to target certain groups for support in different lessons by spending more time with a particular group.

2   Mixing ability — in a mixed-ability group, stronger students can support the less confident ones. It is possible to consider topics that some students may have more experience of, or opinion on, than others. This is a great way of encouraging strong peer support in the class. You can give more able students leadership responsibility in a mixed-ability group.

3   By friendship — there may be times when you want a group to sit with their friends, or peers with whom they share common interests. It is not true that students cannot work effectively with friends and it is good practice to ensure that they can and do when it is appropriate. Working in friendship groups can also offer emotional security to students who may be experiencing stressful situations, or finding things challenging.

Some teachers sit their classes in two horseshoe shapes – one inner horseshoe and one outer – see Figure 10.1. You can then sit the students who need more support at the inner horseshoe. When you want students to work in pairs or groups, you can get the inner horseshoe to turn around and work with the student/s behind them, resulting in mixed-ability groups.

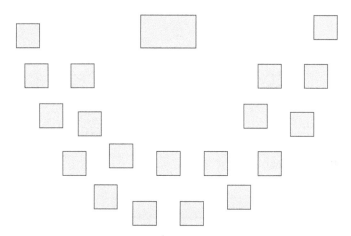

Figure 10.1: Horseshoe classroom layout.

Teacher Tip

The main thing is to keep your seating plan varied and reasonably unpredictable so that your classroom is a dynamic environment. Having more than one seating plan avoids labelling students by always seating them on certain tables.

Make sure that if your class is sitting in groups, all students can see you when you are addressing them. Putting tables at angles to one another, with students sitting on three sides, ensures that no students have their back to you or the whiteboard. See Figure 10.2.

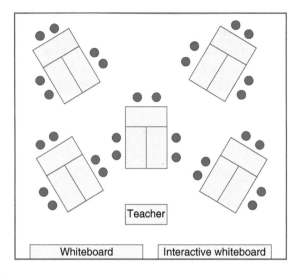

Figure 10.2: Grouped classroom layout.

Using resources to support differentiated learning

Teachers use a wealth of classroom resources to enable differentiated learning. When planning a lesson, you should think carefully about the intended learning outcomes, then different routes to enable students to achieve them. Using classroom resources individually can ensure that all students are able to access the learning in all lessons. In English, differentiation will often be through outcomes, but there are many support resources that can be utilised to improve outcomes for those students that need more support.

LESSON IDEA 10.3: SUPPORTING ALL STUDENTS THROUGH WRITING TASKS

This lesson idea focuses on how to use classroom resources to support all students doing the same directed writing task in order to ensure that the whole class can complete the task. Careful use of these resources will enable you to take the class through the task with each student fully supported.

→

The class have been asked to write a letter of complaint after purchasing an item from a shop which has turned out to be faulty. They should make sure that their letter includes the following information:

- *the name of the item and the date of purchase*
- *what fault has developed and how it inconvenienced you*
- *what you expect the shop to do to compensate for the fault.*

To successfully complete this task, the students will have to think carefully about register, tone, format, structure, use of vocabulary and sentence structure.

Use of classroom resources during the lesson:

- wall displays – to offer key vocabulary to access the content language required for the task, or for appropriate sentence starters and connectives
- interactive whiteboard – to model the formal writing style needed for the task, or to model the thought processes needed to access the task fully
- model answer / scaffold plan – to support those who need help to structure their response effectively
- dictionary – to allow learners to check vocabulary and spelling
- thesaurus – to allow learners to extend and develop their vocabulary.

Stretching and challenging all students

The first question that many new teachers ask is, 'How do we stretch and challenge all students in our class?' Students do not always achieve their full potential; they may find some aspects of a curriculum easy, yet struggle in another. The important thing is never to label students and make assumptions, but to look at each student's progress holistically, considering their educational and social needs. Sometimes poor behaviour in the classroom can be due to frustration or boredom associated with a lack of challenge. Also, students for whom English is a second language can be overlooked when stretching and challenging students. Knowing your students and identifying their potential should be a continuous process over the whole academic year. This is essential to ensure that students are consistently given opportunities to demonstrate their skills and abilities.

The feedback you offer is important when stretching and challenging all students. When a student consistently gets good grades and finds the work set easy, they can become frustrated and switch off as they are not being sufficiently challenged. Writing a comment on a student's work such as 'Excellent – what a superb piece of writing' is not helpful or constructive, as it offers no feedback as to what was effective, or areas of their work that they could extend further. Even when a student is producing top-grade work, they need targets for improvement!

Encouraging students to think in the abstract can be done through effective questioning. Asking *how* rather than *why* stretches students by requiring them to think more deeply. For example, when studying an article with a class, you may ask *what* tone the article is written in, but follow this up with questions about *how* the tone affects the reader's response, or *how* the tone is established.

Teacher Tip

To keep students focused, they must be stretched and challenged. This does not simply mean setting some students more written work; it means changing the nature of the work that you set according to the needs of the individual student. It may be that you will ask them to do further research into a topic, or ask them to make connections between a text they have studied and a text which will require wider reading. You should encourage them to take the initiative and tell you how they would like their work to develop further.

Checking your inclusivity

Look at Figure 10.3 showing a department's inclusivity checklist for reading. In this department, *accommodations* are made where students follow the same curriculum, but individual needs are accommodated through the use of digital technology or by giving extra time, whereas *modifications* are made when the curriculum is adapted to suit the needs of the student. What ideas could you use to make your classroom more inclusive for all students?

Reading accommodations and modifications	
Accommodations checklist	**Modification checklist**
☐ Audio version of book	☐ Content at student's reading level
☐ Audio version of iPad	☐ Highlight key words or phrases
☐ Read aloud setting on iPad	☐ Bold key words
☐ Texts based on interest	☐ Teacher marking key pages or paragraphs with sticky notes
☐ Two textbooks – one at school and one for use at home	☐ Focus on key objectives
☐ Reading aloud text on computer	☐ Questions focus on one or two key concepts
☐ Auditory presentations given with visual examples	☐ Sentence starters
☐ Graphic organiser	☐ Word bank
☐ Extended reading time	☐ Reworded questions to simplify language
☐ Model of completed work provided	☐ Summary of text
☐ Student marking key pages or key paragraphs with sticky notes	

Figure 10.3: Reading accommodations and modifications checklist.

Summary

Now that we have looked at how we can make a classroom more inclusive you will have a good understanding of:

- the importance of knowing your students' individual needs
- the importance of working within school systems and using the support offered
- how classroom layout can be optimised to enhance learning for all
- how you can differentiate the language you use for instruction
- how you can ask questions effectively to differentiate
- how to challenge all students.

Teaching with digital technologies

What are digital technologies?

Digital technologies enable our students to access a wealth of up-to-date digital resources, collaborate locally and globally, curate existing material and create new material. They include electronic devices and tools that manage and manipulate information and data.

Why use digital technologies in the classroom?

When used successfully, digital technologies have the potential to transform teaching and learning. The effective use of technology in the classroom encourages active learning, knowledge construction, inquiry and exploration among students. It should enhance an existing task or provide opportunities to do things that could not be done without it. It can also enhance the role of assessment, providing new ways for students to demonstrate evidence of learning.

New technologies are redefining relationships and enabling new opportunities. But there are also risks, so we should encourage our students to be knowledgeable about and responsible in their use of technology. Integrating technology into our teaching helps prepare students for a future rooted in an increasingly digitised world.

What are the challenges of using digital technologies?

The key to ensuring that technology is used effectively is to remember that it is simply a resource, and not an end in itself. As with the use of all resources, the key is not to start with the resource itself, but to start with what you want the student to learn. We need to think carefully about why and how to use technologies as well as evaluating their efficiency and effectiveness.

If students are asked to use digital technologies as part of their homework, it is important that all students are able to access the relevant technology outside school. A school needs to think about a response to any 'digital divide', because if technology is 'adding value', then all students need to be able to benefit. Some schools choose to make resources available to borrow or use in school, or even loan devices to students.

Safety for students and teachers is a key challenge for schools and it is important to consider issues such as the prevention of cyber-bullying, the hacking of personal information, access to illegal or banned materials and distractions from learning. As technology changes, schools and teachers need to adapt and implement policies and rules.

One of the greatest pitfalls is for a teacher to feel that they are not skilled technologists, and therefore not to try. Creative things can be done with simple technology, and a highly effective teacher who knows very little about technology can often achieve much more than a less effective teacher who is a technology expert. Knowing how to use technology is not the same as knowing how to teach with it.

How digital technologies are re-shaping English teaching

There is a strong argument that today's students are exposed to technology from such a young age that their ability to focus on and absorb information is shaped differently to previous generations, and that using technology in the classroom is a much more realistic reflection of their lives outside the classroom. To ensure that they learn to use their digital skills in a valuable way throughout their lives, we must ensure that their use of digital technologies extends beyond social media, entertainment, surfing the net for easy information and internet shopping. Using digital technologies in the classroom broadens understanding and enables students to use their devices to enhance their learning and reap huge benefits. This is far more relevant use of the equipment that they have and will prepare them more fully for future employment.

And it's not just the students who can benefit. Using digital technologies can help you develop and share resources, assist with marking and offering immediate feedback to students, as well as enabling you to store, share and access data. It is essential that classroom teachers of all ages, across all countries, take steps to embrace technology and successfully integrate digital tools in the curriculum.

Teacher Tip

Make sure that you harness social media. It is part of our students' day-to-day lives and they can follow all sorts of interesting people on Twitter and access a wide range of articles and information. The 140 character limit can also be an exciting way of teaching students to write concisely!

Technology training

Hopefully, your school will offer regular training for teachers who want to develop their use of technology in the classroom. This can often be achieved within the school itself by harnessing the expertise of the IT department or individual teachers who are more technically aware than others. There are also many online courses available to familiarise yourself with technology tools. Many are free and offer great guidance for users who are just beginning.

Teacher Tip

Make sure that you are aware of the training and expertise available in your school and never be afraid to ask for help and guidance when you want to learn something new. In return, ensure that you share your expertise and knowledge when you discover an exciting new digital tool or website.

Recommended technology tools for beginners

It may be helpful at this point to think about how digital tools can support the teaching of English by students doing a variety of things, such as:

- accessing information from a variety of sources and responding to a widening range of texts
- organising and presenting information in a variety of forms
- broadening the range of audiences for their oral and written work
- writing a widening range of texts for a broad range of purposes
- writing for real audiences
- identifying key characteristics and features of texts
- developing understanding of language.

In order to make effective use of digital technologies in your classroom, you need to think carefully about how you can use them to support the learning of your students. Before using new software or devices, you need to be confident that their deployment will aid learning rather than become a distraction. Sharing good practice with colleagues and ensuring that appropriate training is given is fundamental to making the best use of new technologies.

It may be that your school has limited digital resources. If that is the case, as you read this chapter you should consider how you can adapt different ideas to suit the technologies available to you. Putting students in groups to share computers, or modelling working with technologies using a projector and screen can enable you to access technologies even when resources may be more limited. You can also utilise students' own equipment, such as smartphones, to use digital technologies in your lessons. Remember that most mobile phones have video recording capabilities that students can use to record activities.

Figure 11.1 (The SAMR model) is a useful starting point when thinking about effective use of technology in the classroom. It demonstrates the stages followed by teachers as they learn to use digital tools as an increasingly integrated aspect of their teaching.

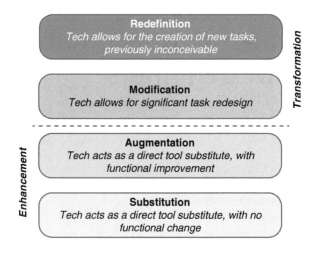

Figure 11.1: The SAMR model.

LESSON IDEA 11.1: USING THE SAMR MODEL

This lesson idea shows you how a traditional English assignment can be adapted using the SAMR model.

Assignment: A discursive composition which would usually be handwritten.

Substitution: A computer replaces the pen.

Augmentation: A computer and online thesaurus are used to improve the writing process.

Modification: The document written using the computer and text-to-speech function is shared on a blog where feedback is received and used to improve the quality of the writing.

Redefinition: Instead of a written assignment, students analyse a discursive topic and devise a presentation using multimedia tools.

Blogging

As English teachers, we want to encourage our students to write, to share their thoughts and feelings, and learn to express them in a way that will interest readers. A great way to do this is to encourage your students to write a blog, either individually or as a class. There are a number of popular blogging platforms available, offering front pages with post updates and blog pages accessed by tabs. Bloggers can post their written work or images, and you can use the homepage for recommended reading lists, setting the latest tasks and activities or homework updates. A comments box will also allow your students to respond to you. This can be a really useful tool in the case of student absence, as it will immediately tell them what they have missed and allow them to post questions.

Cloud-based services

Cloud-based classrooms offer a free suite of tools to teachers. Cloud-based classrooms allow you to set up a classroom online which your students join. You can assign work, collect work, make announcements, mark work and offer feedback, all online. You can work collaboratively with other teachers, or share documents and instructions across several classes. Students can also work collaboratively on pieces of writing and a tool enables you to see at a glance what each individual student has contributed to group work. You can also easily check if students have completed homework or an assignment. You can create a resource page, store marks and grades, and even set up a system where a parent receives an email if a student does not submit an assignment.

☑ LESSON IDEA ONLINE 11.2: COLLABORATIVE CREATIVE WRITING

This lesson idea uses a cloud-based classroom tool to create a piece of creative writing collaboratively.

Online learning platforms

There are a variety of online learning platforms available to teachers. These learning management systems can be used by teachers, students and parents and offer a wide variety of functions. They are controlled by the teacher and designed for educational purposes. On some platforms, for example, the class share a timeline as their homepage, where you can interact with your students and they can interact with each other. You can use these learning platforms to set assignments which students can hand in online and receive feedback. There are some great functions, for example, you can set quizzes to test knowledge and understanding, or you can create a poll to get feedback from your students about a particular lesson, unit of study or assignment. You can also set up a class library to store reading passages, mark schemes, worksheets and other resources.

Creating mind maps

You can use digital tools to create team mind maps. This is highly effective and allows groups of students to share ideas and brainstorm, watching their ideas spread rapidly in front of their eyes. This can be a great way of exploring creative writing ideas, or developing the class's knowledge of a topic for discursive writing.

Wiki

A Wiki is a website that a teacher can create with academic content. The users of the website can edit the site and make changes. A Wiki can be a great way of collaborating with other teachers in your department, or you can create a Wiki for your class. A useful assignment for students to work collaboratively in groups can be to design a Wiki page on a given research topic. Students can be assigned different areas to research and roles within the group. This encourages reflection on learning and discussion of key ideas. There are some excellent websites to help you get started, which clearly explain how to set up and use a Wiki.

Video/Vlogs

Recording students doing presentations is a great way of building up their confidence; many find it far less inhibiting to present to a screen or camera and there are a number of free online tools to enhance screen recordings. Create a YouTube channel for example, to upload class presentations, or to upload videos that you can use with your classes. This can be a very useful tool if you are using a 'flipped classroom' and want your students to watch a particular filmed presentation at home. You can create playlists for different topics and texts, and your students can add to the playlist from their own research on the internet. TED Talks, which can be found on YouTube, are a valuable resource to introduce topics for discursive writing, or to prepare students for their own Speaking and Listening assessments by allowing them to analyse how the speakers use presentational skills effectively. While YouTube can be a useful resource, make sure to supervise your students to ensure that they do not access any inappropriate content.

☑ LESSON IDEA ONLINE 11.3: PRESENTATIONS IN PAIRS

This lesson idea uses a range of digital tools in the preparation of paired student presentations on conspiracy theories or unexplained mysteries. If your school has limited technological resources, the lessons can be flipped so that the research and presentation design are completed at home.

Using digital technologies also allows you to develop skills that support different layers of thinking and learning. Figure 11.2 demonstrates how different uses can encourage learning at every level of Bloom's Taxonomy.

Figure 11.2: Digital Bloom's Taxonomy – a visual Bloom's with appropriate technology tools for teaching and learning collected together.

Teacher Tip

Think about what digital tools you already use in your life or work. Can you think of ways in which you could use those tools in your classroom?

LESSON IDEA 11.4: WRITING IN CONTEXT

Students at secondary and upper-secondary level should learn to adopt appropriate writing styles including newspaper reports, formal speeches and letter writing. There are many ways that you can utilise digital technologies in your lessons to develop appropriate writing styles.

Your students can work in groups to produce a local newspaper, which can include articles and a readers' letter page. Through their contributions, students can do research on local issues, carry out surveys of the class to gather opinions, interview individuals and then write up articles, editorials and letters. The newspapers produced by the different groups can be displayed or stored online. Giving writing a clear sense of purpose and a 'real-life' context is an effective way of preparing students for directed writing tasks. It also makes the process more relevant and allows students to work collaboratively.

It gets easier

You will find that the more you utilise digital technologies in your teaching, the easier it will get. Many technology tools for teaching have similar functions such as drag and drop. Often when you have mastered one tool, it makes the others far more easy to use. As new tools become available you will find it easy to adapt to them, and your own awareness of how technology can be harnessed will increase. Figure 11.3 shows how a teacher can develop technical competence in the classroom through appropriate training and planning.

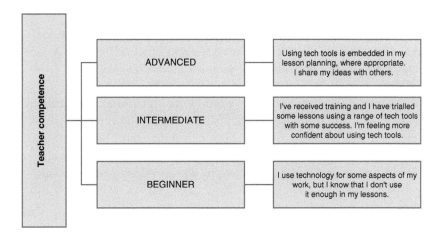

Figure 11.3: The stages of teacher competence in using digital technologies.

Using digital tools to develop language skills

Building vocabulary

There is a wealth of online tools that can replace printed dictionaries and thesauri and enable your students to look up unfamiliar words that they encounter in their reading, or explore new vocabulary to use in their own writing. These tools enable much more efficient ways of researching language and can save time for you and your students. A number of internet tools are free so it is worth doing some research to see which ones you could incorporate into your lessons.

For very quick checking of spelling and definitions, there are word-reference tools which can be mounted on the browser toolbar, while more comprehensive dictionaries can be added to the favourites bar or bookmarked for easy access. For many students the ease of use of these tools will ensure that they take advantage of the opportunities that they offer to increase their vocabulary and improve their English.

Using word clouds to analyse texts

There are many online tools for generating 'word clouds' from texts that you provide. These can be used for a number of purposes when exploring unseen passages with your students. They are a really effective way of looking at informative texts for summary writing, for example. Try starting with a word cloud and asking your students to work out the topic of the text. When developing the skills of selection and synthesis, using a word cloud can help them pick out key words and points. The tools allow you to create images using different fonts, colours and layouts, so you can design them to suit your purposes.

Digital texts

As English teachers, we all want our students to read more widely and view reading as a source of pleasure as well as an important skill. Often technology is cited as an obstacle to getting students to read more, but as an English teacher there are ways that you can use technology to make reading more accessible and ensure that you have books that will suit different tastes and levels of reading skill. Keeping the books available to students up-to-date can be challenging when you are sourcing hard copies, but have you thought about developing an online class library? Many books are now available to download on e-readers, making sourcing a wide range of new reading material much easier and cheaper. Some can be downloaded free of charge, especially classical literature which is out of copyright, and a whole range of unseen passages can be sourced this way.

Audio books and text-to-speech

Some of your students may need greater support to access the texts set for reading comprehension exercises. Learning to pronounce new vocabulary can also be challenging when reading independently. For less confident readers, try using a text-to-speech (TTS) tool, which allows them to hear words that they can't pronounce. TTS increases their reading speed and reduces anxiety about accessing the reading material. You can also access audio books. This type of tool is invaluable and ensures that students don't just brush past words that they don't understand or can't pronounce, leaving them with an incomplete understanding of the text.

Many TTS tools are free and can be downloaded to the desktop, or mounted on the browser toolbar. There are also some e-readers which are free to download.

Story writing

There are several tools for writing stories. Students can create stories and add pictures or music. The stories are then published online so that students can read and review one another's work. This can give story writing a much greater sense of purpose. The stories can be written in different genres or with targeted audiences. Using this kind of digital tool enhances the sense of students becoming actual writers and makes the process of writing stories much more creative and exciting. You can build up a class library of their own books and poems.

Speaking and listening

There are some really exciting possibilities to develop speaking and listening skills through the use of communication tools such as Skype or Facetime. Many teachers have forged links with schools in other countries and arranged Skype interviews between students to allow them to explore other cultures and develop their language skills at the same time. Preparing for the interviews also links in with effective questioning, something explored further in Chapter 7 **Assessment for Learning**.

Teacher Tip

Look back at the lesson ideas for developing narrative and descriptive writing skills in Chapter 6 **Active learning**. These could be developed further using a digital story writing tool.

Summary

In Chapter 11 we have looked at ways in which you can increase your use of digital technologies in your English lessons. Think about:

- what training you would benefit from

- your awareness of the technologies available to you

- how you can plan lessons to increase your use of digital technologies

- what support and expertise is available in your school.

Global thinking 12

What is global thinking?

Global thinking is about learning how to live in a complex world as an active and engaged citizen. It is about considering the bigger picture and appreciating the nature and depth of our shared humanity.

When we encourage global thinking in students we help them recognise, examine and express their own and others' perspectives. We need to scaffold students' thinking to enable them to engage on cognitive, social and emotional levels, and construct their understanding of the world to be able to participate fully in its future.

We as teachers can help students develop routines and habits of mind to enable them to move beyond the familiar, discern that which is of local and global significance, make comparisons, take a cultural perspective and challenge stereotypes. We can encourage them to learn about contexts and traditions, and provide opportunities for them to reflect on their own and others' viewpoints.

Why adopt a global thinking approach?

Global thinking is particularly relevant in an interconnected, digitised world where ideas, opinions and trends are rapidly and relentlessly circulated. Students learn to pause and evaluate. They study why a topic is important on a personal, local and global scale, and they will be motivated to understand the world and their significance in it. Students gain a deeper understanding of why different viewpoints and ideas are held across the world.

Global thinking is something we can nurture both within and across disciplines. We can invite students to learn how to use different lenses from each discipline to see and interpret the world. They also learn how best to apply and communicate key concepts within and across disciplines. We can help our students select the appropriate media and technology to communicate and create their own personal synthesis of the information they have gathered.

Global thinking enables students to become more rounded individuals who perceive themselves as actors in a global context and who value diversity. It encourages them to become more aware, curious and interested in learning about the world and how it works. It helps students to challenge assumptions and stereotypes, to be better informed and more respectful. Global thinking takes the focus beyond exams and grades, or even checklists of skills and attributes. It develops students who are more ready to compete in the global marketplace and more able to participate effectively in an interconnected world.

What are the challenges of incorporating global thinking?

The pressures of an already full curriculum, the need to meet national and local standards, and the demands of exam preparation may make it seem challenging to find time to incorporate global thinking into lessons and programmes of study. A whole-school approach may be required for global thinking to be incorporated in subject plans for teaching and learning.

We need to give all students the opportunity to find their voice and participate actively and confidently, regardless of their background and world experiences, when exploring issues of global significance. We need to design suitable activities that are clear, ongoing and varying. Students need to be able to connect with materials, and extend and challenge their thinking. We also need to devise and use new forms of assessment that incorporate flexible and cooperative thinking.

Thinking globally in the English classroom

As English teachers we develop skills of reading, writing and oracy by selecting texts for study, choosing topics for exploration through writing and discussion and developing communication skills to enable our students to live and work in an increasingly global society. Teachers are often reminded that we are preparing students to work in jobs that have not yet been invented, in companies and fields that do not yet exist, so how do we prepare our students for the futures that they face?

Designing a curriculum that encourages global thinking is often dependent on whole-school policies that require individual departments to consider how they develop global thinking through the curriculum they offer. We are fortunate that, as English teachers, we have a wealth of texts from across the globe to draw upon to ensure that the resources that we use in our teaching truly reflect the increasingly global outlook necessary to educate young people for today's world. We can also choose our own topics for discursive and narrative writing assignments that encourage research into other cultures and perspectives, and that encourage our students to develop the ability to step into someone else's shoes and observe the world through their eyes. These topics can also focus on issues of global concern such as sustainability, climate change, inequality, consumerism and human responsibility.

In this chapter we will consider how we can teach topics to encourage global thinking in our classes while developing the communication skills that students need to meet the learning objectives of the course. We will consider each component of the English course and how, in the delivery of that component, we can develop our students as global thinkers.

A global classroom?

Schools vary widely in their student intake: you may be working in a school where the students are largely from a small locality, or you may be working in an international school where students are drawn from a number of countries around the world. How you introduce your class to global thinking will depend on these factors.

☑ LESSON IDEA ONLINE 12.1: WRITING IN AN AUTOBIOGRAPHICAL STYLE

This lesson idea, using an online article, involves developing personal profiles with your students through developing the written style of autobiography. The Meera Syal article is just an example, other autobiographical articles can be used. This will enable you to discover where your students are from, and where their parents and grandparents are from.

Asking students to read out and discuss their autobiography is a great way of illustrating how, in one class, they can get a sense of themselves as being part of a global society.

If you find that students in your class come from a range of different nations, ask them to include what aspects of their lives are different because they no longer live in their home country. What customs and traditions do they miss, what have they brought with them? Ask them to explain their celebration days.

Teacher Tip

You could broaden the discussion out at this point and consider the way that we are influenced by other countries in our everyday lives. What food do they like to eat? What music do they listen to? What films do they watch? What books do they read? Work out how much of what we do each day is dependent on goods and services that are provided from different countries around the world.

Topic 1 – inequality

To introduce a topic and encourage students to think more widely, starting with their own experiences and then broadening their perspective, is a useful starting point.

Start with the statement 'Life isn't fair!' and ask students to consider in groups what they think is fair or unfair in their own lives. Many are likely to focus on family situations and siblings, or life at school and friendships. They may consider material possessions or the amount of freedom they get as teenagers. Ask each group to come up with a list of things that they consider to be unfair in their own lives and offer feedback to the rest of the class. Then consider how many common areas there are and whether their perception of fairness is influenced by any particular factors.

Speaking and listening

When students have considered 'Life isn't fair' in their own lives, put students into groups and put an image like Figure 12.1 on the whiteboard, then take the class through a Visible Thinking routine:

- See – they spend five minutes looking at the image and describing what they can see.
- Think – they spend five minutes looking at the image and explaining what they think about any aspect of it.
- Wonder – they spend five minutes looking at the image and wondering what questions it raises about the world they live in.

It is important that students keep strictly to the required stage of thinking throughout the process. Each group should make bullet-pointed notes at each stage.

At the end of the process, ask different groups to read out their bullet points for each stage and open up a discussion about inequality in the world today.

Then go back to the students' initial consideration of fairness in their own lives and ask them if their views have changed, or have been refined in the light of the Visible Thinking routine.

Teacher Tip

At this point, you may ask students to reflect on their contribution to the Visible Thinking routine. Each group could offer one another feedback on the contribution made to the process. This can be an excellent way of ensuring that students are given an equal voice and also understand the importance of listening and drawing others into the discussion.

Figure 12.1: Favela image for a Visible Thinking routine.

Writing

The Visible Thinking routine could lead on to a piece of discursive writing entitled "Life isn't fair!' How far do you agree with this view?' You could advise students to use a similar process when considering the statement – start with their own perspective, then widen it out to consider it from a global perspective.

To incorporate directed writing into this topic, you could ask students to work in groups as fundraisers for a project on inequality they feel passionately about, either in their local area or internationally. They could do a variety of tasks, including designing leaflets, writing letters requesting support, or writing articles to raise awareness.

Figure 12.1 shows the dividing wall between luxury apartment blocks and the favelas of Rio De Janeiro. You could use the image to inspire a piece of narrative writing entitled 'The wrong side of the wall'. Students would have to decide which side is the wrong side!

Reading

Continuing with the topic of 'Life isn't fair', you can also link it to selected fiction reading passages where students have to view events through the perspective of the characters. When choosing reading passages, try to make them an appropriate length – about 750-850 words – and make sure that they stand alone or with a very brief introduction. You can use passages from past papers where appropriate.

☑ LESSON IDEA ONLINE 12.2: ANALYSIS OF A FICTION PASSAGE TO EXPLORE PERSPECTIVE

This lesson idea is based on a reading passage where characters face difficult economic circumstances through no fault of their own. Students look at how perspective is conveyed through the writer's use of language and structure. The short story *Coconuts* by David Iglehart is just one example of a text that could be used in this lesson.

Topic 2 – environmental awareness

This is a wide ranging topic which again can be explored through many of the components of the English Language syllabuses. It has many cross-curricular links with subjects such as geography and global perspectives, and you will find that students have a good knowledge base which they can use to develop discursive writing skills.

A good start is to find out what students know, and what aspects of environmental awareness interest them most. Start by listing what they are interested in and finding out what they already know. Hopefully they will suggest some or all of the following:

- animal conservation
- pollution and health

- recycling vs. waste
- littering the land and seas
- carbon footprints.

When they have decided on a list of sub-topics, you can offer them choices to explore them further. Follow the same pattern suggested for the topic of inequality.

A good starting point may be the question 'Could we do more to protect our planet?' Again, suggest that students start by considering what they could do, as an individual, to protect the planet, then widen it out to consider more global issues.

Ask students to start by thinking about the following questions:

Figure 12.2

When students have discussed these questions, ask them to widen out their discussion to consider their family, then local community or school, and whether there are ways in which they could consider the planet more through being a member of those communities. Remind them that this is a discursive topic so there should be different sides to the arguments put forward.

They should then widen it out to think about global issues – what could all the people of the world be doing, or stop doing, to preserve the health of the planet? Is there an argument suggesting that we already do enough, or that there are other priorities?

Teacher Tip

This is a really effective way of structuring a discursive composition – start personally, then consider their wider community, then consider the topic from a global perspective.

Speaking and listening

Figures 12.3 and Figure 12.4 are suggested images that you could use for a Visible Thinking routine, which should follow the same process as outlined in Topic 1. You could also use them to stimulate discussion in speaking and listening activities. Think about the topics that could be explored using these images.

Figure 12.3

Figure 12.4

Writing

LESSON IDEA 12.3: HOLDING A CLASS DEBATE

Give your class the discursive title: 'Should governments spend money on conserving wild animals?'

Split the class into groups. Ask half the groups to argue in favour of governments supporting wild animals and half the groups to argue against. Tell them to move beyond their own perspective and try to view the topic from another viewpoint.

Hold a debate with the class before asking them to write an argumentative response giving both sides of the argument before expressing their viewpoint.

There are many opportunities for developing writing on this topic. Getting pairs of students to design their own webpage, or writing magazine articles to persuade young people to become more environmentally aware are both tasks that will prepare students for the writing styles they need to develop.

Reading

This topic lends itself to non-fiction texts. There are a number of passages that can be used to practise summary writing skills, as well as texts where students respond to the writer's viewpoint by creating their own piece of writing in response to the text.

Teacher Tip

When exploring a topic like this, you could consider getting involved in wider educational projects, such as the ones organised by the British Council. Search online for the 'Partner Schools Global Network, British Council'. In this project, you team up with a partner school in a different country to work on a virtual project. There are a number of interesting global topics on the website and full details of how your school can get involved.

Topic 3 – news reporting

The way that we receive news has changed exponentially in the last two decades and we are now exposed to news sources from all around the world. This offers us a range of opportunities to explore how news is reported as part of our English curriculum. This topic focuses on written news – both in newspapers and online. It provides a range of activities designed to make students understand how reporting adapts to locality and circumstance and how perspective changes depending on the writer's viewpoint and purpose.

Before you begin, find out how many of your students read newspapers or online news sites. What interests them in the news? Are they interested in news that affects them and their locality, or do they take a wider interest in international news reporting?

Suggested introductory activities on news reporting:

- **Listening for details** Ask students to listen carefully as you read aloud a story from the day's newspaper. Then hand out a worksheet with questions asking about details from the story. Students or groups respond to the questions to allow you to see if they were listening carefully.
- **News-mapping** Stick a country map on the classroom wall. Give groups of students a ball of string and articles from different local newspapers or websites. Ask them to put up the stories around the map and use the string to match each story to the location on the map where the story takes place. How does the style and language of an article differ when it is written for local readers about a local concern?
- **News skimming** Provide students with a list of things to find on the front page of today's newspaper. They might hunt for grammar-related terms (a present-tense verb, a past-tense verb, a proper noun, an abbreviation, a colon or a list separated by commas), or you might let students work in small groups to hunt for as many nouns (or proper nouns, or verbs) they can find in a story or on the front page. This activity can be developed to distinguish between fact and opinion, or to spot bias.
- **Scanning the page** Provide a copy of a news story for this activity that teaches the skill of 'scanning for information'. Ask students to scan the article to retrieve specific information. Then ask them to reorganise and synthesise the information before writing it up in their own words.
- **Local, national or international?** To develop your students' understanding of the different types of news stories, create a board divided into three sections. Invite students to bring in news stories that might fit into each of the three sections. News of the locality should be posted in the 'Local' section. News of interest to the whole country should be placed in the 'National' section, and world news items should be posted in the 'International' section. Ask students to decide whether there is a difference in the types of stories that fit into each section.

LESSON IDEA 12.4: SPOT THE DIFFERENCE
Give your students three articles covering the same story from
three different news sources. Ask them to spot any differences in
the way that the story is reported. They should look for evidence
of bias or for emphasis placed on different aspects of the story and
decide what may have determined these differences.

Creating a newspaper

When you have introduced your students to the world of news
reporting, and they have an understanding of how news reporting
works locally, nationally and internationally, they can develop their own
newsroom.

Each day, newspaper editors around the world must make decisions
about which stories they will publish. Stories make it into newspapers
for many different reasons. Invite students to look at the stories that
have made the front page of a national newspaper during the last few
days and to talk about why each of those stories made headlines. Among
the reasons students might come up with are these:

- Immediacy — the story is of interest to readers in that moment.
- Relevance — the story is about a concern of national interest.
- Magnitude — the story is about something affecting large numbers
  of people.
- Unexpectedness — the story is about something that has occurred
  without warning.
- Impact — the story will affect a large number of readers.
- VIP — the story is about an important person or celebrity.
- Drama — the story is about a major conflict or struggle.
- Achievement — the story is celebrating an achievement,
  breakthrough.

When students have done sufficient research into how newspapers
balance the types of stories, and what tends to be front page news,
they can design their own newspaper and write their own stories
using the same principles.

Teacher Tip

To develop your students' speaking and listening skills, one of the topics we have explored in this chapter will give them plenty of scope for exploring their subject fully and devising a researched and knowledgeable presentation.

Summary

In Chapter 12 we have explored a topic-based approach to encouraging our students to become global thinkers.

- A topic-based curriculum allows you to cover all the components of the syllabus, including coursework, examination preparation and speaking and listening.

- Teaching your students to be global thinkers widens their perspectives, which increases their empathy as both readers and writers.

- Visible Thinking routines support self-regulated learning processes. You can follow this structure with different topics that encourage global thinking.

13 Reflective practice

Dr Paul Beedle, Head of Professional Development Qualifications, Cambridge International

'As a teacher you are always learning'

It is easy to say this, isn't it? Is it true? Are you bound to learn just by being a teacher?

You can learn every day from the experience of working with your students, collaborating with your colleagues and playing your part in the life of your school. You can learn also by being receptive to new ideas and approaches, and by applying and evaluating these in practice in your own context.

To be more precise, let us say that as a teacher:

- You **should** always be learning
  to develop your expertise throughout your career for your own fulfilment as a member of the teaching profession and to be as effective as possible in the classroom.
- You **can** always be learning
  if you approach the teaching experience with an open mind, ready to learn and knowing how to reflect on what you are doing in order to improve.

You want your professional development activities to be as relevant as possible to what you do and who you are, and to help change the quality of your teaching and your students' learning – for the better, in terms of outcomes, and for good, in terms of lasting effect. You want to feel that 'it all makes sense' and that you are actively following a path that works for you personally, professionally and career-wise.

So professional learning is about making the most of opportunities and your working environment, bearing in mind who you are, what you are like and how you want to improve. But simply experiencing – thinking about and responding to situations, and absorbing ideas and information – is not necessarily learning. It is through reflection that you can make the most of your experience to deepen and extend your professional skills and understanding.

Approaches to learning and teaching First Language English

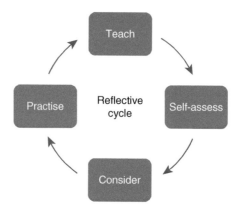

Figure 13.1

In this chapter, we will focus on three *essentials* of reflective practice, explaining in principle and in practice how you can support your own continuing professional development:

1 **Focusing** on what you want to learn about and why.
2 **Challenging** yourself and others to go beyond description and assumptions to critical analysis and evaluation.
3 **Sharing** what you are learning with colleagues – to enrich understanding and enhance the quality of practice.

These essentials will help you as you apply and adapt the rich ideas and approaches in this book in your own particular context. They will also help you if you are, or are about to be, taking part in a Cambridge Professional Development Qualification (Cambridge PDQ) programme, to make the most of your programme, develop your portfolio and gain the qualification.

1 Focus

In principle

Given the multiple dimensions and demands of being a teacher, you might be tempted to try to cover 'everything' in your professional development but you will then not have the time to go beneath the surface much at all. Likewise, attending many different training events will certainly keep you very busy but it is unlikely that these will simply add up to improving your thinking and practice in sustainable and systematic ways.

Teachers who are beginning an organised programme of professional learning find that it is most helpful to select particular ideas, approaches and topics which are relevant to their own situation and their school's priorities. They can then be clear about their professional learning goals, and how their own learning contributes to improving their students' learning outcomes. They deliberately choose activities that help make sense of their practice with their students in their school and have clear overall purpose.

It is one thing achieving focus, and another maintaining this over time. When the going gets tough, because it is difficult either to understand or become familiar with new ideas and practices, or to balance learning time with the demands of work and life, it really helps to have a mission – to know why you want to learn something as well as what that something is. Make sure that this is a purpose which you feel genuinely belongs to you and in which you have a keen interest, rather than it being something given to you or imposed on you. Articulate your focus not just by writing it down but by 'pitching' it to a colleague whose opinion you trust and taking note of their feedback.

In practice

- Plan
  What is my goal and how will I approach the activity?

  Select an approach that is new to you, but make sure that you understand the thinking behind this and that it is relevant to your students' learning. Do it for real effect, not for show.

- Monitor
  Am I making progress towards my goal; do I need to try a different approach?

  Take time during your professional development programme to review how far and well you are developing your understanding of theory and practice. What can you do to get more out of the experience, for example by discussing issues with your mentor, researching particular points, and asking your colleagues for their advice?

- Evaluate
  What went well, what could have been better, what have I learned for next time?

  Evaluation can sometimes be seen as a 'duty to perform' – like clearing up after the event – rather than the pivotal moment in learning that it really is. Evaluate not because you are told you have to; evaluate to make sense of the learning experience you have been through and what it means to you, and to plan ahead to see what you can do in the future.

This cycle of planning, monitoring and evaluation is just as relevant to you as a professional learner as to your students as learners. Be actively in charge of your learning and take appropriate actions. Make your professional development work for you. Of course your professional development programme leaders, trainers and mentors will guide and support you in your learning, but you are at the heart of your own learning experience, not on the receiving end of something that is cast in stone. Those who assist and advise you on your professional development want you and your colleagues to get the best out of the experience, and need your feedback along the way so that if necessary they can adapt and improve what they are devising.

2 Challenge

In principle

Reflection is a constructive process that helps the individual teacher to improve their thinking and practice. It involves regularly asking questions of yourself about your developing ideas and experience, and keeping track of your developing thinking, for example in a reflective journal. Reflection is continuous, rather than a one-off experience. Being honest with yourself means thinking hard, prompting yourself to go beyond your first thoughts about a new experience and to avoid taking for granted your opinions about something to which you are accustomed. Be a critical friend to yourself.

In the Cambridge PDQ Certificate in Teaching and Learning, for example, teachers take a fresh look at the concepts and processes of learning and challenge their own assumptions. They engage with theory and models of effective teaching and learning, and open their minds through observing experienced practitioners, applying new ideas in practice and listening to formative feedback from mentors and colleagues. To evidence in their assessed portfolio how they have learned from this experience, they not only present records of observed practice but also critical analysis showing understanding of how and why practices work and how they can be put into different contexts successfully.

The Cambridge PDQ syllabuses set out key questions to focus professional learning and the portfolio templates prompts to help you. These questions provide a framework for reflection. They are open-ended and will not only stimulate your thinking but lead to lively group discussion. The discipline of asking yourself and others questions such as 'Why?' 'How do we know?' 'What is the evidence?' 'What are the conditions?' leads to thoughtful and intelligent practice.

In practice

Challenge:

- Yourself, as you reflect on an experience, to be more critical in your thinking. For example, rather than simply describing what happened, analyse why it happened and its significance, and what might have happened if conditions had been different.
- Theory – by understanding and analysing the argument, and evaluating the evidence that supports the theory. Don't simply accept a theory as a given fact – be sure that you feel that the ideas make sense and that there is positive value in applying them in practice.
- Convention – the concept of 'best practice(s)' is as good as we know now, on the basis of the body of evidence, for example on the effect size of impact of a particular approach on learning outcomes. By using an approach in an informed way and with a critical eye, you can evaluate the approach relating to your particular situation.

3 Share

In principle

Schools are such busy places, and yet teachers can feel they are working on their own for long periods because of the intensity of their workload as they focus on all that is involved in teaching their students. We know that a crucial part of our students' active learning is the opportunity to collaborate with their peers in order to investigate, create and communicate. Just so with professional learning: teachers learn best through engagement with their peers, in their own school and beyond. Discussion and interaction with colleagues, focused on learning and student outcomes, and carried out in a culture of openness, trust and respect, helps each member of the community of practice in the school clarify and sharpen their understanding and enhance their practice.

This is why the best professional learning programmes incorporate collaborative learning, and pivotal moments are designed into the programme for this to happen frequently over time: formally in guided learning sessions such as workshops and more informally in opportunities such as study group, teach meets and discussion, both face-to-face and online.

In practice

Go beyond expectations!

In the Cambridge PDQ syllabus, each candidate needs to carry out an observation of an experienced practitioner and to be observed formatively themselves by their mentor on a small number of occasions. This is the formal requirement in terms of evidence of practice within the portfolio for the qualification. The expectation is that these are not the only times that teachers will observe and be observed for professional learning purposes (rather than performance appraisal).

However, the more that teachers can observe each other's teaching, the better; sharing of practice leads to advancement of shared knowledge and understanding of aspects of teaching and learning, and development of agreed shared 'best practice'.

So:

- open your classroom door to observation
- share with your closest colleague(s) when you are trying out a fresh approach, for example an idea in this book
- ask them to look for particular aspects in the lesson, especially how students are engaging with the approach – pose an observation question
- reflect with them after the lesson on what you and they have learned from the experience – pose an evaluation question
- go and observe them as they do the same
- after a number of lessons, discuss with your colleagues how you can build on your peer observation with common purpose, for example lesson study
- share with your other colleagues in the school what you are gaining from this collaboration and encourage them to do the same
- always have question(s) to focus observations and focus these question(s) on student outcomes.

Pathways

The short-term effects of professional development are very much centred on teachers' students. For example, the professional learning in a Cambridge PDQ programme should lead directly and quickly to changes in the ways your students learn. All teachers have this at heart – the desire to help their students learn better.

The long-term effects of professional development are more teacher-centric. During their career over, say, 30 years, a teacher may teach many thousand lessons. There are many good reasons for a teacher to keep up-to-date with pedagogy, not least to sustain their enjoyment of what they do.

Each teacher will follow their own career pathway, taking into account many factors. We do work within systems, at school and wider level, involving salary and appointment levels, and professional development can be linked to these as requirement or expectation. However, to a significant extent teachers shape their own career pathway, making decisions along the way. Their pathway is not pre-ordained; there is room for personal choice, opportunity and serendipity. It is for each teacher to judge for themselves how much they wish to venture. A teacher's professional development pathway should reflect and support this.

It is a big decision to embark on an extended programme of professional development, involving a significant commitment of hours of learning and preparation over several months. You need to be as clear as you can be about the immediate and long-term value of such a commitment. Will your programme lead to academic credit as part of a stepped pathway towards Masters level, for example?

Throughout your career, you need to be mindful of the opportunities you have for professional development. Gauge the value of options available at each particular stage in your professional life, both in terms of relevance to your current situation – your students, subject and phase focus, and school – and the future situation(s) of which you are thinking.

14 | Understanding the impact of classroom practice on student progress

Lee Davis, Deputy Director for Education, Cambridge International

Introduction

Throughout this book, you have been encouraged to adopt a more active approach to teaching and learning and to ensure that formative assessment is embedded into your classroom practice. In addition, you have been asked to develop your students as meta-learners, such that they are able to, as the academic Chris Watkins puts it, 'narrate their own learning' and become more reflective and strategic in how they plan, carry out and then review any given learning activity.

A key question remains, however. How will you know that the new strategies and approaches you intend to adopt have made a significant difference to your students' progress and learning? What, in other words, has been the impact and how will you know?

This chapter looks at how you might go about determining this at the classroom level. It deliberately avoids reference to whole-school student tracking systems, because these are not readily available to all schools and all teachers. Instead, it considers what you can do as an individual teacher to make the learning of your students visible – both to you and anyone else who is interested in how they are doing. It does so by introducing the concept of 'effect sizes' and shows how these can be used by teachers to determine not just whether an intervention works or not but, more importantly, *how well* it works. 'Effect size' is a useful way of quantifying or measuring the size of any difference between two groups or data sets. The aim is to place emphasis on the most important aspect of an intervention or change in teaching approach – the **size of the effect** on student outcomes.

Consider the following scenario:

Over the course of a term, a teacher has worked hard with her students on understanding 'what success looks like' for any given task or activity. She has stressed the importance of everyone being clear about the criteria for success, before students embark upon the chosen task and plan their way through it. She has even got to the point where students have been co-authors of the assessment rubrics used, so that they have been fully engaged in the intended outcomes throughout and can articulate what is required before they have even started. The teacher is happy with developments so far, but has it made a difference to student progress? Has learning increased beyond what we would normally expect for an average student over a term anyway?

Here is an extract from the teacher's markbook.

Student	Sept Task	Nov Task
Katya	13	15
Maria	15	20
Joao	17	23
David	20	18
Mushtaq	23	25
Caio	25	38
Cristina	28	42
Tom	30	35
Hema	32	37
Jennifer	35	40

Figure 14.1

Before we start analysing this data, we must note the following:

- The task given in September was at the start of the term – the task in November was towards the end of the term.
- Both tasks assessed similar skills, knowledge and understanding in the student.
- The maximum mark for each was 50.
- The only variable that has changed over the course of the term is the approaches to teaching and learning by the teacher. All other things are equal.

With that in mind, looking at Figure 14.1, what conclusions might you draw as an external observer?

You might be saying something along the lines of: 'Mushtaq and Katya have made some progress, but not very much. Caio and Cristina appear to have done particularly well. David, on the other hand, appears to be going backwards!'

What can you say about the class as a whole?

Calculating effect sizes

What if we were to apply the concept of 'effect sizes' to the class results in Figure 14.1, so that we could make some more definitive statements about the impact of the interventions over the given time period? Remember, we are doing so in order to understand the size of the effect on student outcomes or progress.

Let's start by understanding how it is calculated.

An effect size is found by calculating 'the standardised mean difference between two data sets or groups'. In essence, this means we are looking for the difference between two averages, while taking into the account the spread of values (in this case, marks) around those averages at the same time.

As a formula, and from Figure 14.1, it looks like the following:

$$\text{Effect size} = \frac{\text{average class mark (after intervention)} - \text{average class mark (before intervention)}}{\text{spread (standard deviation of the class)}}$$

In words: the average mark achieved by the class *before* the teacher introduced her intervention strategies is taken away from the average mark achieved by the class *after* the intervention strategies. This is then divided by the standard deviation[1] of the class as a whole.

---

[1] The standard deviation is merely a way of expressing by how much the members of a group (in this case, student marks in the class) differ from the average value (or mark) for the group.

Inserting our data into a spreadsheet helps us calculate the effect size as follows:

	A	B	C
1	**Student**	September Task	November Task
2	Katya	13	15
3	Maria	15	20
4	Joao	17	23
5	David	20	18
6	Mushtaq	23	25
7	Caio	25	38
8	Cristina	28	42
9	Tom	30	35
10	Hema	32	37
11	Jennifer	35	40
12			
13	Average mark	23.8 = AVERAGE (B2:B11)	29.3 = AVERAGE (C2:C11)
14	Standard deviation	7.5 = STDEV (B2:B11)	10.11 = STDEV (C2:C11)

Figure 14.2

Therefore, the effect size for this class $= \dfrac{29.3 - 23.8}{8.8} = 0.62$
But what does this mean?

Interpreting effect sizes for classroom practice

In pure statistical terms, a 0.62 effect size means that the average student mark **after** the intervention by the teacher, is 0.62 standard deviations above the average student mark **before** the intervention.

We can state this in another way: the post-intervention average mark now exceeds 61% of the student marks previously.

Going further, we can also say that the average student mark, post-intervention, would have placed a student in the top four in the class previously. You can see this visually in Figure 14.2 where 29.3 (the class average after the teacher's interventions) would have been between Cristina's and Tom's marks in the September task.

This is good, isn't it? As a teacher, would you be happy with this progress by the class over the term?

To help understand effect sizes further, and therefore how well or otherwise the teacher has done above, let us look at how they are used in large-scale studies as well as research into educational effectiveness more broadly. We will then turn our attention to what really matters – talking about student learning.

Effect sizes in research

We know from results analyses of the Program for International Student Assessment (PISA) and the Trends in International Mathematics and Science Study (TIMMS) that, across the world, a year's schooling leads to an effect size of 0.4. John Hattie and his team at The University of Melbourne reached similar conclusions when looking at over 900 meta-analyses of classroom and whole-school interventions to improve student learning – 240 million students later, the result was an effect size of 0.4 on average for all these strategies.

What this means, then, is that any teacher achieving an effect size of greater than 0.4 is doing better than expected (than the average) over the course of a year. From our example above, not only are the students making better than expected progress, they are also doing so in just one term.

Here is something else to consider. In England, the distribution of GCSE grades in Maths and English have standard deviations of between 1.5 and 1.8 grades (A★, A, B, C, etc.), so an improvement of one GCSE grade represents an effect size of between 0.5 and 0.7. This means that, in the context of secondary schools, introducing a change in classroom practice of 0.62 (as the teacher achieved above) would result in an improvement of about one GCSE grade for each student in the subject.

Furthermore, for a school in which 50% of students were previously attaining five or more A★–C grades, this percentage (assuming the effect size of 0.62 applied equally across all subjects and all other things being equal) the percentage would rise to 73%.

Now, that's something worth knowing.

What next for your classroom practice? Talking about student learning

Given what we now know about effect sizes, what might be the practical next steps for you as a teacher?

Firstly, try calculating effect sizes for yourself, using marks and scores for your students that are comparable, e.g. student performance on key skills in maths, reading, writing, science practicals, etc. Become familiar with how they are calculated so that you can then start interrogating them 'intelligently'.

Do the results indicate progress was made? If so, how much is attributable to the interventions you have introduced?

Try calculating effect sizes for each individual student, in addition to your class, to make their progress visible too. To help illustrate this, let us return to the comments we were making about the progress of some students in Figure 14.1. We thought Cristina and Caio did very well and we had grave concerns about David. Individual effect sizes for the class of students would help us shed light on this further:

Student	September Task	November task	Individual Effect Size
Katya	13	15	0.22*
Maria	15	20	0.55
Joao	17	23	0.66
David	20	18	-0.22
Mushtaq	23	25	0.22
Caio	25	38	1.43
Cristina	28	42	1.54
Tom	30	35	0.55
Hema	32	37	0.55
Jennifer	35	40	0.55

_____

* The individual effect size for each student above is calculated by taking their September mark away from their November mark and then dividing by the standard deviation for the class – in this case 8.8.

Figure 14.3

If these were your students, what questions would you now ask of yourself, of your students and even of your colleagues, to help you understand why the results are as they are and how learning is best achieved? Remember, an effect size of 0.4 is our benchmark, so who is doing better than that? Who is not making the progress we would expect?

David's situation immediately stands out, doesn't it? A negative effect size implies learning has regressed. So, what has happened, and how will we draw alongside him to find out what the issues are and how best to address them?

Why did Caio and Cristina do so well, considering they were just above average previously? Effect sizes of 1.43 and 1.54 respectively are significantly above the benchmark, so what has changed from their perspective? Perhaps they responded particularly positively to developing assessment rubrics together. Perhaps learning had sometimes been a mystery to them before, but with success criteria now made clear, this obstacle to learning had been removed.

We don't know the answers to these questions, but they would be great to ask, wouldn't they? So go ahead and ask them. Engage in dialogue with your students, and see how their own ability to discuss their learning has changed and developed. This will be as powerful a way as any of discovering whether your new approaches to teaching and learning have had an impact and it ultimately puts data, such as effect sizes, into context.

Concluding remarks

Effect sizes are a very effective means of helping you understand the impact of your classroom practice upon student progress. If you change your teaching strategies in some way, calculating effect sizes, for both the class and each individual student, helps you determine not just *if* learning has improved, but by *how much*.

They are, though, only part of the process. As teachers, we must look at the data carefully and intelligently in order to understand 'why'. Why did some students do better than others? Why did some not make any progress at all? Use effect sizes as a starting point, not the end in itself.

Ensure that you don't do this in isolation – collaborate with others and share this approach with them. What are your colleagues finding in their classes, in their subjects? Are the same students making the same progress across the curriculum? If there are differences, what might account for them?

In answering such questions, we will be in a much better position to determine next steps in the learning process for students. After all, isn't that our primary purpose as teachers?

Acknowledgements, further reading and resources

This chapter has drawn extensively on the influential work of the academics John Hattie and Robert Coe. You are encouraged to look at the following resources to develop your understanding further:

Hattie, J. (2012). *Visible Learning for Teachers – Maximising Impact on Learning*. London and New York: Routledge.

Coe, R. (2002). *It's the Effect Size, Stupid. What effect size is and why it is important.* Paper presented at the Annual Conference of The British Educational Research Association, University of Exeter, England, 12–14 September, 2002. A version of the paper is available online on the University of Leeds website.

The Centre for Evaluation and Monitoring, University of Durham, has produced a very useful effect size calculator (available from their website). Note that it also calculates a confidence interval for any effect size generated. Confidence intervals are useful in helping you understand the margin for error of an effect size you are reporting for your class. These are particularly important when the sample size is small, which will inevitably be the case for most classroom teachers.

15 | Recommended reading

For a deeper understanding of the Cambridge approach, refer to the Cambridge International website (www. cambridgeinternational.org/teaching-and-learning) where you will find the following in-depth guides:

Implementing the curriculum with Cambridge; a guide for school leaders.

Developing your school with Cambridge; a guide for school leaders.

Education briefs for a number of topics, such as active learning and bilingual education. Each brief includes information about the challenges and benefits of different approaches to teaching, practical tips, lists of resources.

Getting started with... These are interactive resources to help to explore and develop areas of teaching and learning. They include practical examples, reflective questions and experiences from teachers and researchers.

For further support around becoming a Cambridge school visit cambridge-community.org.uk.

There is a wealth of reading that can help you develop your skills and knowledge as an English teacher. If you would like to develop your understanding of the theories and strategies explored in this book, try accessing some of the recommendations for wider reading listed below.

There are some excellent blogs exploring the challenges facing English teachers and the latest strategies for the classroom teacher:

Collins English Language Teaching Blog.

The Confident Teacher, Alex Quigley.

Reading all the Books, Jo Facer.

Learning Spy, David Didau.

For resources to make your English classroom more global, visit the website:

Global Dimension.

For exploring the development of oracy skills, visit the website:

The 21 Trust.

For developing strategies for teaching literacy:

Didau, D. (2014) *The Secret of Literacy: Making the Implicit, Explicit.* Carmarthen: Independent Thinking Press.

Lemov, D. (2016) *Reading Reconsidered: A Practical Guide to Rigorous Literacy Instruction.* San Francisco: Jossey Bass.

For becoming a more reflective teacher:

Green, A. (2011) *Becoming a Reflective English Teacher.* London: Open University Press.

For developing your students' potential:

Dweck, C. (2012) *Mindset: How You Can Fulfil Your Potential.* London: Robinson.

For developing active learning strategies:

Sevilla, M. (2012) *Active Learning in the 21st-century Classroom.* CreateSpace.

Siberman, M. (1996) *Active Learning: 101 Strategies to Teach any Subject.* London: Pearson.

Suggested strategies for teaching English grammar:

Aitken, R. (2002) *Teaching Tenses: Ideas for Presenting and Practising Tenses in English.* Sussex: ELB Publishing.

Edwards, C. and Willis, J. (2005) *Teachers exploring Tasks in English Language Teaching.* London: Palgrave Macmillan.

Penston, T. (2005) *A Concise Grammar for English Language Teachers.* Co. Wicklow: TP Publications.

For taking a more global view of teaching, considering what we can learn from the education systems of five high performing countries:

Crehan, L. (2016) *Cleverlands: The Secrets Behind the Success of the World's Education Superpowers.* London: Unbound.

A valuable resource for extra reading on meta-learning in diverse classroom environments:

Watkins C (2015) *Meta-Learning in Classrooms.* The SAGE Handbook of Learning. Edited by Scott D. and Hargreaves E. London: Sage Publications Ltd.

Index